WE REMEMBER
THE HOLOCAUST

EUROPE 1938–39

• Principal Cities
■ Concentration Camps (1933–45)

WE REMEMBER
THE HOLOCAUST

DAVID A. ADLER

Henry Holt and Company · New York

Published by Henry Holt and Company, Inc.,
115 West 18th Street, New York, New York 10011.
Published in Canada by Fitzhenry & Whiteside Limited,
195 Allstate Parkway, Markham, Ontario L3R 4T8.

Library of Congress Cataloging-in-Publication Data
Adler, David A.
    We remember the Holocaust.
    Bibliography.
    Includes index.
    Summary: Discusses the events of the Holocaust and
includes personal accounts from survivors of their
experiences of the persecution and the death camps.
    ISBN 0-8050-0434-3
    1. Holocaust, Jewish (1939–1945)—Juvenile literature.
2. Holocaust, Jewish (1939–1945)—Personal narratives—
Juvenile literature.   3. Jewish children—Europe—
Juvenile literature.   [1. Holocaust, Jewish (1939–1945).
2. Holocaust, Jewish (1939–1945)—Personal narratives.
3. World War, 1939–1945—Jews]   I. Title.
D810.J4A328   1989   940.53′15′03924   87-21139

Henry Holt books are available at special discounts
for bulk purchases for sales promotions, premiums,
fund-raising, or educational use. Special editions
or book excerpts can also be created to specification.

        For details contact:

    Special Sales Director
    Henry Holt and Company, Inc.
    115 West 18th Street
    New York, New York 10011

Designed by Victoria Hartman
Printed in the United States of America
10   9   8   7   6   5   4   3

Contents

Preface

Much of what occurred during the dark years 1933 to 1945 seems too horrible to imagine. Atrocities were large scale and commonplace, especially after the beginning of the Second World War. While Allied and Axis soldiers fought on battlefields, the Nazis waged a war against unarmed people. They killed Russian prisoners of war, Communists, Gypsies, homosexuals, Serbs, cripples, Jehovah's Witnesses, the mentally ill, and beggars. And they killed Jews, an estimated six million Jews. The Nazis planned the total destruction of the Jewish people. The murder of these Jews became known as the Holocaust.

I was born shortly after the end of the Holocaust, in the midst of America's "baby boom." As a young child I was surrounded by survivors. I saw people in the bakery, in the delicatessen, and at the beach with numbers tattooed on their arms. I had friends with no aunts, uncles, or grandparents. I grew up knowing about the Six Million.

Today's generation—my children's generation—is being raised in a different world, a world in which many young people don't know about the Holocaust. There are adults

Betty Adler's German
passport photo, 1935.

who prefer to forget about the Holocaust. Some even claim it never happened. The many people I interviewed for this book are witnesses. There *was* a Holocaust, and its victims were doctors, lawyers, tailors, factory workers, store owners, teachers, and students—fathers, mothers, and children—people like us.

My mother was born in Germany and raised in Austria. She remembers: "When Hitler came to power in Germany, we were already in Austria. My teacher called me to the front of the class, pointed out my blond hair and blue eyes, and said, 'You see, this is what a typical Aryan looks like.' She was trying to show the class how ridiculous Nazi policy was. They all knew I was Jewish." A week after Hitler and the Nazis entered Austria, my mother escaped to Holland, then went to England, Mexico, and finally the United States. She often told me, "It could happen anywhere, even here. When you see it coming, don't wait. Leave. Don't let yourself become tied to material things. Just leave."

Now I have children of my own. While I always intended to talk to them about Hitler, the Nazis, and the Six Million, I was not prepared when, five years ago, my seven-year-old son asked, "What happened in the Holocaust?" I had intended to wait, to tell him years later, when he would be older. I answered him briefly. I told him it was a tragic, recent period in our history when six million Jews were killed in Europe simply out of hatred. And I began working on this book in an attempt to answer his question more fully.

This book began as a history, but I wanted my son to know more than names, dates, places, a tally of the people killed. I wanted him to learn about the Holocaust not only within its historical context, but also as the Jews of Europe knew it, as one personal tragedy on top of another. So I

Preface

Most of the people quoted in this book were children or teenagers when the events they described occurred. Remembering these events and talking about them was difficult, but they spoke so we would remember the sufferings of an entire people, so we would remember the millions murdered, among them their own parents and grandparents, their own sisters and brothers. They spoke because they hope, as I do, that there will never again be another Holocaust, that once we know where hatred can lead us, we will learn not to hate.

1

"I remember people carrying around tremendous bundles of money"

Ernest Honig, 1946.

Ernest Honig remembers: "It was early evening when the train stopped and the doors opened. As I came off the train, I saw on the left huge chimneys belching forth thick black smoke. There was a strange smell, like burning the feathers off a chicken before it was cooked. I didn't know that the smoke and the smell were not from chickens. I didn't know, until I found out later on, that I was smelling our own flesh, our own families burning."

Leo Machtingier remembers: "It was hell. It was worse than hell. When it ended, all my family was gone, my parents, grandparents, sisters, brother, uncles, aunts, cousins, all of them."

Esther Klein remembers: "What I saw was horror upon horror upon horror."

They remember the Holocaust, years of discrimination, torture, and agony for the Jews living in Europe—years of mass killings. Six million Jews were killed, men and women, children, even babies. This was to be genocide, the destruction of an entire people. The principle reason for it was not to gain land or property, but simply to kill.

Esther Klein in Czechoslovakia, 1946.

Most were not random killings, but were carefully planned and carried out by the Nazis in death camps built for their efficiency—camps built to kill a great number of people as quickly as possible and at low cost.

Nazi persecution of Jews began in 1933, but the history of prejudice that led to it began long before then. For hundreds of years European Jews were often mistreated and attacked, forced to pay special taxes, forbidden to own land, to work at certain occupations, or to be citizens of certain countries. At times Jews were required to wear cloth patches identifying them as Jews. They were expelled from Spain, Portugal, England, and France. Even some church leaders spoke out against the Jews. For centuries, in times of trouble, Jews were convenient scapegoats, wrongly blamed for wars, plagues, and poverty. And after the First World War the Jews were blamed for Germany's troubles too.

After the end of the First World War—known at the time as the Great War—the leaders of Germany were forced to sign the Treaty of Versailles, which blamed Germany for having caused the war. Germany lost land. It was no longer permitted to maintain a navy, and the size of its army was limited. Germany was forced to pay billions of dollars to other nations for the suffering the war had caused.

During the early 1920s inflation made German money almost worthless. Before the Great War it took a little more than four German marks to buy one American dollar. By November 1923 it took more than 500 billion German marks to buy a dollar, and with every passing hour German money became worth even less. The German national bank had hundreds of presses printing money day and night. German money had so little value that people used it as notepaper.

Children built towers with bundles of the almost worthless money.

Netti Golde Dessau lived in Frankfurt am Main, one of Germany's larger cities and an important center of Jewish life. She remembers the inflation of the early 1920s: "It was an awful time. My mother was a widow living on a pension. Every afternoon the first thing we looked at in the newspaper was the value of the mark. One day my mother told me that on the way to school I should stop and order some coal. I was late, so I did it on the way home instead. On the way to school I would have gotten about one hundred kilograms of coal. By the afternoon, for the same money, all we got was maybe seventy kilograms."

Netti Golde Dessau, 1941.

Edith Busek also lived in Frankfurt am Main. She was a young girl in 1923. She remembers: "Every day my father looked at the index to see what happened to the mark. At one time friends of my family sold valuable pictures. Gosh, they thought, when will we ever see such prices again? But later the idea was to hold on to merchandise, not money. Oh, I remember people carrying around tremendous bundles of money."

Arno Rhein lived in Zurich, Switzerland. He remembers: "My father went on a business trip to Germany, and every night he wrote in a diary how many million marks he got that day for each Swiss franc he exchanged. For many years we looked at those numbers in amazement."

A new currency, the *Rentenmark*, was issued in 1923. Payments due under the Treaty of Versailles were reduced. The German economy was saved. But there was more economic trouble ahead. In 1929 the Great Depression began in the United States. It quickly spread to Europe and left millions of Germans out of work and hungry.

During these desperate times more and more Germans

Arno Rhein, 1936.

3

were willing to listen to the hate-filled talk of a former soldier named Adolf Hitler. Hitler claimed that true Germans were superior to other people and must retake the land they had lost in the Great War. They must conquer new land from neighboring countries to add *Lebensraum*, living space, for the German people. They must rid the country of the people who he claimed caused all Germany's troubles—the Communists and the Jews.

Adolf Hitler was born in Austria on April 20, 1889. He was a bright but lazy student and never graduated from high school. August Kubizek, a minor Austrian government official, first met Hitler in 1904, when they were both teenagers. They were close friends and shared a room in Vienna for several weeks in 1908. Kubizek later wrote that Hitler had a quick temper. And even as a young man Hitler was openly anti-Semitic.

In 1913 Adolf Hitler moved to Germany. He hardly worked at all until the outbreak of the Great War, when he enlisted in the German Army. In 1916 Hitler's leg was wounded, and in October 1918 he suffered an eye injury. He was still in a military hospital when the war ended in November 1918, but Hitler could not accept the terms of the ceasefire. He felt that the Germany he loved had been humiliated.

In 1919 Adolf Hitler began his campaign for power. He joined the German Workers' Party, a small group of men who gathered to talk about politics and to listen to speeches about rebuilding Germany. They spoke about the state's responsibility to find work and food for its citizens. And they spoke about their hatred of Jews. They called Jews "vermin" and insisted that lists of where each Jew in Germany lived be kept by the government. They insisted that Jews be removed from all jobs in government, newspapers, and movie-making.

Deutsche Arbeiter=Partei (D. A. P.)
Ortsgruppe München   Abteilung:

Mitgliedskarte

für _____

München, den _____ 1. Jan. 1920

Nr. **660**   Für den Arbeitsausschuß:

_____   _____
Schriftwart

Diese Karte gilt als Ausweis bei geschlossenen
Versammlungen

Early German Workers' Party card, 1920.

Within a few months Hitler was one of the leaders of the German Workers' Party. The party was soon renamed the *Nationalsozialistische Deutsche Arbeiterpartei* (the National Socialist German Workers' Party), but it was generally called the Nazi party.

Hitler spoke often of his hatred of the Jews. He stood on street corners and in smoke-filled beer halls. He would shout and wave his fists, and stir his listeners. He called Jews "the personification of the devil, the symbol of all evil." He said, "By defending myself against Jews, I am doing the work of the Lord."

Netti Golde Dessau remembers when she first heard Hitler speak: "He was an enormously strong speaker and really had a way of arousing people. But with his 'superman' idea and with blaming the Jews for everything, we thought he was *meshuga*, crazy. . . . I always felt if I did nothing wrong, nothing would happen to me. I couldn't understand the idea that people would persecute us just because we were Jewish."

Adolf Hitler.

Al Feuerstein with his
sister, 1937.

Henriette Kaplan lived as a young child in Frankfurt am Main. She remembers: "People left their windows open, and when I walked by, I often heard their radios playing. When I heard Hitler speak, I knew who it was. I was terrified by his voice."

Al Feuerstein lived in Czechoslovakia, and he remembers sitting by the radio and listening to Hitler speak: "He said the German nation suffered poverty, starvation, and hunger because of the Jews. He called us parasites. Hitler would scream and yell, and the radio would shake, or seem to, when he spoke. People were frightened to listen to him. Terror would reach out to us through the radio."

The Nazis had their own flag, a black swastika inside a white circle and sewn on red cloth. And beginning in 1920 the Nazis had their own brown-uniformed soldiers, called the SA, or *Sturmabteilungen* (storm troopers). They fought in the streets with Communists and other enemies of Nazism. They attacked Jews in restaurants and in synagogues.

In 1919 a new German government had been formed, the Weimar Republic. It was a democratic government. According to its constitution, the government was formed in freedom to establish peace at home and abroad. The powers of the new government were to come from the people of Germany.

Men and women twenty years and older elected a president and representatives to the *Reichstag*, or parliament. The president appointed various ministers, as well as the chancellor, who set government policy. But the president's appointments needed the approval of a majority of the *Reichstag*. And there was a second, less important, house in the German government, the *Reichsrat*. In it were representatives from each of the German states.

Hitler's Brown Army, 1927.

Elections were held in January 1919 and June 1920, and in both elections the Nazi party did not win a seat in the *Reichstag*. The Nazis were eager for power. In Munich, on November 8, 1923, they attempted a *Putsch*, a revolt, to take control by force of Bavaria, a state in southern Germany. They failed. Eighteen Nazis were killed. Hitler and several other Nazi officers were arrested for high treason, tried, and sentenced. While Hitler was in jail, he wrote *Mein Kampf* ("My Struggle"), which outlined his plans for a greater, more powerful Germany. Hitler was released from jail after nine months.

After their failed *Putsch*, the Nazis changed their tactics. They began to use Germany's democratic process to gain power. They campaigned hard for votes, and as conditions in Germany worsened, the Nazis steadily gained seats in the government.

Hitler leaving jail, Landsberg, 1924.

Siegfried Sonneberg, 1938.

In 1925 Hitler formed a new group of uniformed Nazi soldiers, the *Schutzstaffel* (protection squad), generally known as the SS. They wore black uniforms and black boots and had metal images of a small skull pinned to their caps. They vowed "loyalty and bravery and obedience unto death" to Hitler, their *Führer* (leader).

Siegfried Sonneberg lived in Somborn, Germany, a small town near Frankfurt am Main. During Hitler's campaigns for votes, he often saw SA and SS troops marching at rallies. "There was always some Nazi leader at the rally trying to get everyone excited by shouting about the Jews, that we were thieves, that we were sucking their blood. We walked away real fast."

Edith Busek lived in Frankfurt am Main. She remembers: "Groups of people assembled at street corners, and in the center was always a young rabble-rouser making anti-Semitic speeches. They sang bloodcurdling songs day and night. I remember the refrain from one of the songs, 'Oh, what a glorious day it will be *wenn Judenblut vom messer spritzt*—when Jewish blood spurts from the knife.' " And she remembers listening to the radio and hearing Hitler speak: "He had an awful, yelling voice. He made hysterical speeches which sent shivers down my spine."

In July 1932 elections were held in Germany. The Nazis won 230 of the 608 seats in the *Reichstag*, more than any other party. Hitler was offered the position of vice chancellor. But Hitler controlled the party with the largest representation in the *Reichstag*. He demanded to be named chancellor. The president, Paul von Hindenburg, refused. He didn't trust Hitler or the Nazis.

New elections were held in November 1932. The Nazi party was the most powerful of the more than thirty political parties in Germany. But Hindenburg still enjoyed great personal popularity, and he defeated Hitler for the presidency. Even though the Nazis had received thirty-three percent of the votes, after the election Hindenburg appointed someone outside the Nazi party as chancellor.

A Nazi campaign poster. The text reads, "Workers, vote for the front-soldier Hitler!"

Von Hindenburg and Hitler.

9

Manfred Fulda, 1938.

The appointee did not have the support of the *Reichstag*. On January 28, 1933, the president relented and appointed Adolf Hitler to be chancellor of Germany. Hitler agreed to abide by Germany's democratic principles. But it soon became clear that Hitler was not satisfied to be head of his country's government. He would be Germany's absolute ruler, its dictator.

Rabbi Dr. Manfred Fulda lived in the German city of Fulda. He remembers the day Hitler was named chancellor: "My father said to my mother, my sisters, my brother, and me, *'Deutschland ist kein Platz mehr für Juden*—Germany is no longer a place for Jews. We are leaving tonight, and we are leaving everything behind, our house, our business, everything. We are leaving tonight to save our lives.' We left that night, right after the local Nazis' torchlight parade celebrating Hitler's appointment. We went by train to Kehl, and from there we walked across the border into France; but we were caught and arrested by the French border guards. A few weeks later there was a trial. We were found guilty of illegal entry into France and sent back to Germany. When we returned, we were worse off than before. We had committed the terrible 'crime' of trying to leave Germany without the proper papers."

But some Jews still felt secure in Germany. Helga Lowenthal Greenbaum remembers: "My father's family had been in Germany since the seventeenth century. My father was a veteran of the First World War, and he said, 'They wouldn't do anything to us. I fought for Germany.' He felt Germany was his homeland."

Four weeks after Hitler was named chancellor, on February 27, 1933, the *Reichstag*, the German parliament building, was set on fire. It was an impressive building topped by a large glass dome with copper framework. The *Reichstag* was built between 1884 and 1894 with money spoke with witnesses, with survivors of the persecution, the labor camps, and the death camps. But while this book, like many written on the Holocaust, is based on the testimony of survivors, it must be remembered that most European Jews did *not* survive.

In the Jewish community, especially in the New York area, there are many Holocaust survivors. I was led to the people I interviewed by my family and friends and by representatives of various survivor groups, most notably Sydney Mandelbaum of Second Generation and Alfred Lipson of the Holocaust Resource Center at Queensboro Community College. I followed up on many newspaper and magazine articles, and in one instance I even used a magnifying glass to read the address on a "My Name Is . . ." button worn by a survivor in a published photograph.

The first interviews were only with survivors of the camps, but later I interviewed people who remembered pre-Nazi Germany, as well as a few children of survivors, the second generation.

We met, sometimes in my home or office, but most often in their homes. The survivors I spoke with have rebuilt their lives. Among them are teachers, a school administrator, lawyers, a social worker, an artist, a furrier, a chemist, jewelers, a designer, store owners, and businessmen and businesswomen. Many are proud parents and grandparents. After we spoke, I transcribed their statements. I sent each survivor a copy of the quotations I planned to use in the book for his or her approval. Then the statements and the text were reviewed by other survivors and expert historians.

At first this book was to be illustrated only with photographs from public archives. But I wanted to be sure the reader identified closely with the witnesses and victims of prejudice and persecution. So I asked the people interviewed for copies of photographs of them at or about the times they spoke of in this book. Fortunately many such photographs were available.

Some of the photographs of survivors reproduced here were sent to relatives overseas before the war. Others belong to survivors who escaped with some of their possessions. Some photographs were taken soon after liberation.

A few of the survivors I spoke with returned home soon after they were freed. Some of them found a few of their things, including photographs. They had hoped to find family and friends who survived. Sometimes they did.

Unfortunately the quality of some of the photographs is poor. They are all old, and most of them, including many selected from public archives, were taken by amateurs.

Some of the interviews lasted a few hours. Many of the people quoted here were interviewed more than once. Often the interviews ended with "I can't tell it all. It's just too much. It's too painful." That's how I feel. I do not attempt to describe all the pain and horror of that time. *We Remember the Holocaust* is not meant to be the only book a young person will read about the Holocaust. It's meant to be an introduction. The glossary and chronology are meant to supplement as well as to clarify the text. Therefore there are events, people, places, and things listed there that are not included in the body of the book.

It is now more than forty years since the death camps were liberated and more than fifty years since *Kristallnacht*. Survivors who for many years would not speak of their experiences are now willing to talk. They want others to know what they, at one time, were so desperate to forget.

The *Reichstag* in flames,
February 27, 1933.

France gave Germany in payment for losses suffered in the
Franco-Prussian War of 1870. Above the main entrance to
the building was the inscription, "To the German People."
Sometime during the night the glass dome collapsed. The
large central room where the parliament met was completely burned.

It was widely believed that the Nazis set the fire, but they blamed others for it and used the fire as an excuse to pass laws "for the protection of the German people." With these new laws the German people lost many of their civil rights. The Nazis controlled what was being published in newspapers, magazines, and books. Meetings were forbidden. People could be arrested and jailed without trial.

Soon after Hitler came to power, prison camps were set up to hold people opposed to Nazism in "protective custody." In March 1933, shortly after the *Reichstag* fire, Dachau was established by Heinrich Himmler, leader of the SS, as a "model" camp. At the camp there were thirty-two wooden barracks in two rows, all surrounded by an electrified fence. Any prisoner caught walking toward the fence was shot. Camps such as Dachau, in which the enemies of Nazism were concentrated, became known as concentration camps. Labor and death camps set up later followed in many ways the brutal example set by Dachau and the other early concentration camps.

Helga Lowenthal Greenbaum lived in Aschaffenburg, Germany. She remembers: "My friend's father was one of

Helga Lowenthal Greenbaum.

Dachau watchtower, 1933.

the first prisoners at Dachau. This was early in 1933. I don't remember why he was taken there, but I do remember when he was sent back. It was four weeks later, and he was sent back in a box."

Within six months all political parties except the Nazis were outlawed. The Gestapo (Nazi secret police), the SA, and the SS began to hunt and either arrest or kill Hitler's enemies.

On May 10, 1933, the Nazis began an assault of a different kind. In Berlin an estimated forty thousand people watched as five thousand German students marched behind cars and trucks loaded with books. The students carried lit torches, and they sang Nazi and college songs. The president of the student organization, wearing a Nazi uniform, declared that they had gathered to burn un-German books. As the books written by Jews and others were thrown into the fire, another student called out the names of the authors: "Sigmund Freud! Erich Maria Remarque! Heinrich Heine! Thomas Mann! Emil Ludwig!" The crowd cheered. Dr. Joseph Goebbels, Nazi minister of popular enlightenment and propaganda, announced, "Jewish intellectualism is dead," and again the crowd cheered. That night books were also burned in Munich, Frankfurt am Main, Kiel, and elsewhere in Germany. Millions of books were burned because either the author was considered an enemy of Nazism or the theme of the book was not considered suitable.

The same day, in New York City, thousands of people watched as an estimated hundred thousand marchers protested German anti-Semitism. Fifty thousand marched in Chicago, and twenty thousand more in Philadelphia. Even children shouted "Down with Hitler!" But the shouts were not heard in Germany.

German schools eliminated all parent and teacher groups.

Books considered to be harmful to the German state are burned in Berlin, May 10, 1933.

Julius Rosenzweig's passport and identity photo, about 1938.

They rewrote textbooks to teach children to love Hitler and the Nazis. They even rewrote fairy tales. In the Nazi version of the story, Sleeping Beauty was the German nation, and the handsome prince who woke her with a kiss was Adolf Hitler.

Only two youth groups were allowed—the Hitler Youth, for boys, and the League of German Girls. Both groups taught children to spy and report on enemies of Nazism, including their own parents.

Julius Rosenzweig was a teenager in the 1930s. He lived in Frankfurt am Main. He remembers: "There were plenty of Nazis, plenty of Jew haters, but also plenty of people who just went along. There was pressure put on gentile boys to join Hitler Youth. There were signs outside classrooms—'This entire class belongs to Hitler Youth except these shirkers'—and they were listed."

Tirzah Rothschild, as a child in the 1930s, lived with her family in Hamburg, Germany. She remembers: "We had a little wooden house in the country, in Hummelsbüttel, where we went for summer vacations. When there was a shortage of some foods in Hamburg, one of our neighbors in Hummelsbüttel offered to sell us a few eggs, a little butter, and some vegetables. On a chilly day in the fall I took a train to visit her and to get the available food items. We were sitting, talking in the kitchen. Suddenly she looked at the clock and said, 'You'd better leave soon.' I was a bit surprised, as it was still early and the trains back to Hamburg ran quite frequently. 'No, it's not the trains,' she said. 'My son will be home soon. He's in the Hitler Youth, and if he finds you here, it will not be good for you or for me!' "

Tirzah Rothschild's identity card, 1938. Note that "Sarah" was added to her name.

Just about everything done in business and on farms in Germany needed to be approved by the government. Though the German people lost many of their rights, they were at work again. Within six years there were almost ten million new jobs. But the new jobs were mostly making the tools of war—guns, bullets, tanks, and bombers.

While Germany was rebuilding its military strength, Hitler told the German people they were "founders of culture," a "master race" superior to all other groups: superior to blacks, Gypsies, Poles, Jehovah's Witnesses, homosexuals, and especially to Jews. Under Hitler, prejudice and discrimination became public policy.

2

"They wanted everyone to know who the Jews were"

Sidney Adler with his father on the deck of the *Stuttgart*, June, 1929.

Sidney Adler and his father on a tour bus in Berlin, Germany, 1929. Sidney Adler is seated, fourth from left. His father is second from left.

Sidney Adler traveled to Germany with his father in 1929 and again in 1930. "People don't realize how strong Jewish life was in Germany before Hitler. In 1929 we traveled from New York to Bremen, Germany, on the *Stuttgart*, a German boat. There was an extra chef on board to prepare kosher meals for whoever wanted them. When we were seated near the captain, my father told the head steward that as religious Jews we wore yarmulkes on our heads when we ate, and he asked for a less prominent table. The steward was a German. The whole crew was German. He

told my father to stay where we were. 'People should respect you for your religion,' he said.

"We went to visit relatives and we traveled throughout Germany. There were many beautiful synagogues and kosher hotels and restaurants. Even in America, many of the kosher foods we bought for Passover were prepared in Germany."

But Jewish life in Germany deteriorated quickly. During 1933, the first year of the Nazi regime, Jewish judges and lawyers were shut out of German courts. Jewish doctors could no longer work in certain German hospitals. Jewish teachers, bankers, and railroad workers were fired. Jews were removed from service in the army and navy. And the number of Jewish students in high schools and colleges was severely limited.

Henni Prager Sonneberg lived in Wenings, Germany. She remembers spring 1933: "My father was a member of the town council. He had been a first lieutenant in the German Army in the First World War. When the town wanted to build a memorial to the war dead, he got them the steel. He helped with the casting. And he was the first Jew in Wenings to be beaten, the first to be locked up."

Henni Prager Sonneberg's father and brother were beaten in March 1933. "We had a large picture window in our house. Hoodlums, members of the *Arbeitslager* [government work crew] broke the window with two by fours. They found my brother sleeping downstairs and beat him. He fought back. They didn't know a Jew could fight back. And they got pleasure from beating my father, a quiet, middle-aged Jew."

Clara Wachter Feldman lived in a small German town during the early years of Nazi rule. "In the middle of the school year of 1933, our class was given a new teacher, a

Henni Prager Sonneberg's passport photograph, 1934.

Clara Wachter Feldman, 1947.

Nazi party member. The first day he came in, he said, 'I understand we have a Jew pig in our classroom.' Then he said, 'Now we will see how much pain a Jewish pig can endure.' He had me put out my hand, and he hit me with a stick. I don't know how many times he hit me. I don't remember the pain. But I do remember the laughter of the other children."

Henriette Kaplan remembers: "I was told by Jewish friends who lived near Nuremberg that they were taken by the Nazis to a park and forced to pull weeds out with their teeth. This happened soon after Hitler came to power." And she remembers what happened to her several years later in Frankfurt am Main: "I was out mailing letters, and a small boy of seven carrying a stick told me, 'Don't you know that Jews must be beaten?' and he struck me on the back several times. I was furious because I knew I couldn't do anything."

The Nazis issued orders that a general boycott be carried out on April 1, 1933, against Jewish shops, Jewish-made goods, and Jewish doctors and lawyers. The orders urged that the boycott be carried out in "complete calm and with absolute discipline," that Germans "not harm a hair on a Jew's head." The orders stressed the need for Nazi party members "to stand in blind obedience, as one man, behind our leadership."

There were worldwide protests and a boycott of German goods. On March 31, 1933, Dr. Joseph Goebbels told a large crowd of Nazi supporters, "Jewish trade throughout Germany will be paralyzed tomorrow." And he declared that if the anti-German protests did not stop, the boycott would be resumed "until German Jewry has been annihilated." His speech was interrupted by shouts from the audience: "Hang them! Hang them!"

A kiosk in Berlin announces the boycott of Jewish-owned stores.

On April 1, 1933, SS and SA soldiers stood outside Jewish-owned stores, carrying signs urging Germans not to go in. Signs posted throughout the country instructed Germans, "Defend yourselves! Do not buy from Jews." The

The sign reads, "Germans! Wake up! Don't buy from Jews!"

Fred Erlebacher, right, as a member of a U.S. Army intelligence unit, 1945.

word *Jude* (Jew) and Jewish stars were painted on the doors and windows of the stores. Jewish children were not allowed in class.

Fred Erlebacher worked in an iron-and-wood supply house in Baisingen, Germany, a small village near Lahr. He remembers the boycott: "Some people we knew, and were friends the day before, came in wearing brown uniforms. They no longer recognized us. They only knew we were Jews. They yelled at us and insulted us. When a few brave people walked into our store, they were yelled at and called 'Friends of the Jews.'"

Netti Golde Dessau remembers: "There was a young Jewish doctor I knew. She worked in a very poor, non-Jewish section of the city, mostly for free. Before the boycott she said, 'If the people I'm helping here are standing in front of my door with pickets, I'm not staying one day longer.' And they were there." A short while later her friend left Germany and moved to Palestine, the small Middle Eastern country that later became the Jewish state of Israel.

Hilda Bondi remembers the boycott: "My class was on a trip of a few days in the mountains. We all had to return home. The Nazis wanted people to see which children were taken out of the class. They wanted everyone to know who the Jews were."

During the next few years, many Germans refused to buy from Jewish-owned stores. There were anti-Jewish riots. Books written by Jews were thrown into the streets and burned. Jews Not Wanted signs were posted along roads and in stores and restaurants.

Officials throughout the country, eager to show their support of Nazi policy, made their own decrees against Jews. They tried to force Jews out, so their towns could be made *judenrein*, free of Jews. More and more Jews moved to the large cities.

Tirzah Rothschild lived in Hamburg, Germany. She remembers when she saw *Juden Unerwünscht*—Jews Not Wanted—signs: "They appeared all over, in food stores, clothing stores, and department stores. It wasn't the law yet that Jews be forbidden to enter these stores. The owners put up such signs to impress others that they were good Nazis. I remember when I saw those signs I felt sad, scared, and angry."

There were some protests outside Germany, and in July 1933, during an interview, Hitler responded, "I would be only too glad if the countries which take such a great interest in Jews would open their gates to them. It is true we have made discriminatory laws, but they are directed not so much against the Jews, but for the German people, to give economic opportunity to the majority."

Nazi discrimination against the Jews was not reserved only for the living. Any street named after a Jew was renamed. A monument to Heinrich Heine, a Jew and one of

Hilda Bondi with her father, 1927.

A Jewish cemetery desecrated with swastikas.

Lena Mandelbaum, 1940.

Germany's most popular writers, was removed. The monument to Jacob Herz, a great doctor who had served Germany during two wars, was destroyed. A hundred thousand Jewish soldiers had fought in the German Army in the Great War, less than twenty years earlier. Thirty-five thousand had died. Now the names of the Jewish soldiers who died were scratched off German memorials to the war dead.

Jewish children were no longer allowed in public schools. And in public schools a course in "scientific anti-Semitism," the "scientific" hatred of Jews, was taught to every student.

According to the Nuremberg Laws of September 1935, Jews were no longer citizens of Germany. They were not even allowed to fly a German flag. Jews were not allowed to marry non-Jews nor have any non-Jewish woman under the age of forty-five work in their homes.

Fred Erlebacher was arrested for violating the Nuremberg Laws. "I was accused of being with a German girl. The Gestapo came to my place of business and arrested me. It's true, she looked German. She had long blond braids. But she was a Jewish girl, and I told them that. They checked it out. When they found out it was true, they released me. That girl is my wife now."

Lena Mandelbaum was a young child in Germany at the time. She remembers: "My father was in the wholesale fruit business. His partner was not Jewish. He took over the business. Then he lied and said my father stole from him, and he took our apartment. My parents were taken to jail. Soon after that my sisters, brothers, and I were thrown out of school."

Helga Lowenthal Greenbaum remembers: "My brother's bar mitzvah was in 1937. That Friday I was working for my father, and a registered letter came to the office. The letter withdrew permission for my father to have a business. Of course, I didn't show it to my parents until after the bar mitzvah. I didn't want to ruin the celebration. After that my father just wasn't the same. He was still a young man, and he had no work."

The effects of Nazi anti-Jewish policy were felt far beyond Germany. Anti-Semites throughout the world were encouraged by the Nazis. Anti-Jewish laws were passed in Hungary. Jews there lost their jobs, their homes, their rights as citizens. In Romania there were anti-Jewish student riots. Jewish students were kept out of colleges. High taxes were imposed on Jewish businesses. Jews were attacked. In Poland there were anti-Jewish boycotts and riots in the large cities, including such centers of Jewish life as Vilna and Warsaw. In small Polish towns and villages, peasants carrying clubs and rocks attacked Jews.

Thousands of Jews left Poland for British-controlled Palestine. But the Arabs there protested the arrival of the Jews. They became violent and destroyed Jewish property. They attacked and killed Jews.

Arthur Rubin lived in Derecske, Hungary, in the 1930s. "I remember at the young age of five or six years walking to school or to synagogue, and all of a sudden kids in the courtyard would say, 'Hey, you're a Jew.' I remember being beaten and coming home with a bloody nose. It was particularly unwise to walk on the streets during Easter and Christmas holidays. On those holidays the name-calling and the Jew-beatings were carried out with more zeal, with more passion than at other times. This hatred and hostility was a reflection, a mirror image, of the adult population."

Cecilia Bernstein was a young child in the 1930s and lived in a small town in Hungary. She remembers: "Police with long black feathers in their hats rode on horses through the streets. We ran from them. They beat us, and no one could stop them."

Alfred Lipson lived in Radom, in central Poland, during

Arthur Rubin, 1943.

Cecilia Bernstein, 1946.

23

Class photograph, Radom, Poland, 1936. Alfred Lipson is in the front row, fourth from left. Only seven of those pictured here survived the war.

Leah Goldberg, 1946.

the mid 1930s. He remembers: "There were roving gangs in the streets. We were beaten many times. Once, I was in a movie theater with my mother. She was wearing a fur coat. When we left the theater, we found that anti-Semitic hoodlums sitting behind us in the theater had slit my mother's coat with razor blades."

Leah Goldberg remembers growing up in Poland: "Before Passover my gentile friends weren't allowed to play with us. Their parents said Jews kill gentile children and use their blood to make matzos. 'No,' I told them. 'I saw them bake matzo. They use just flour and water. If they used blood, the matzo would be red.' "

Abraham J. Goldberg remembers being a young boy in Poland: "I was once surrounded by six fellows, and one of them said, 'We're going to kill a Jew today.' I ran for my life."

Anti-Semitism was on the rise in Austria, Greece, Yugoslavia, Italy, and France. Even in the United States.

Cantor Moshe Ehrlich was born in Vienna, Austria. He remembers: "Anti-Semitism was rampant. Just as an example of it, on Good Friday, Holy Thursday, and Easter

Abraham Goldberg's class photograph, 1932.

Sunday I was warned by my parents, 'Don't go out, because Jews will be beaten up.' This was before Hitler marched into Austria. The people would come home from church, and any Jew they could find, they would beat up."

In the United States many anti-Jewish groups were formed, including the German-American Bund, the Silver Shirts, and the Christian Front. They publicized their views on radio and in leaflets and magazines.

In the United States and elsewhere only a small minority of the people declared themselves to be anti-Semites. But they were a loud minority. Almost everyone else was quiet.

3

"I heard marching boots everywhere"

Walter Straus, 1938.

Hitler had plans for a new Germany. He would extend his country's borders. He would create a giant empire, and that meant war. Hitler was preparing for it.

Germany's preparations were no secret. German industry was busy making the tools of war. The German Navy and Air Force were being rebuilt. Hundreds of thousands of men were being added to the army each year. This was all against the terms of the Treaty of Versailles. Winston Churchill, then a member of the British House of Commons, knew what all this meant. In 1937 he warned of a coming "hideous catastrophe." His warnings were ignored.

At first Hitler claimed he wanted only to unite Europe's German-speaking people. In March 1938, Hitler declared that Austria, a neighboring German-speaking country, was a part of Germany. When German soldiers marched into that country to annex it as part of greater Germany, many of the Austrian people cheered. They greeted the German Army with their arms stretched out in the Nazi salute.

In 1938 Walter Straus lived in Baden bei Wien, Austria. He remembers the very warm greeting many Austrians

gave the invading Germans: "We had a Jewish guest from Munich the day the German Army marched into Austria. The next day my father had to go on a business trip. I was in the car when our guest drove Dad to the railway station in Vienna, about ten miles away. People must have assumed we were connected with the invasion. There we were, three Jews in a German car with German plates, and

Army Day, Nuremberg, 1937.

Hitler is greeted by enthusiastic followers on National Labor Day, May 1, 1934.

Edith Rhein, 1936.

people all along our route to the station were smiling at us and giving us the Nazi salute."

Edith Rhein also lived in Baden bei Wien. She too remembers the welcome given to the Nazis when they marched into Austria: "By the next morning our neighbors had hung Nazi flags from just about every window."

A few days later was the Jewish holiday of Purim. The holiday celebrates the Jewish victory over Haman, a prime minister of ancient Persia. Haman intended to kill every Jew in the kingdom, as described in the Book of Esther, *"mena'ar v'ad zakain, taf venashim*—the young and the old, small children and women."

Edith Rhein remembers Purim, 1938: "We had certain canned foods put way for special occasions—peas and asparagus, and pineapple, which was a real delicacy then in Europe. Mutti [Mother] took all the cans from the pantry and opened them for Purim. There was no reason to save them anymore. We knew we had to leave. Three days later we left Austria."

Nazi police followed the German Army into Austria, and within days Jews lost their rights as citizens. German SS kicked and spit at Jews. They forced them to clean the streets and public toilets, to crawl on the ground and eat grass, to run in circles until they collapsed.

Many Austrians watched the spectacle and laughed. Thea Sonnenmark lived in Vienna. She remembers: "At the end of March 1938, as my father went to open his grocery store, the SA gave him a toothbrush and ordered him to scrub the street. Some of his non-Jewish customers came by, and when they saw my father there, they laughed and jeered. These were customers of long standing. He considered them to be his friends."

Erika Weihs was born in Vienna. She never expected to

Thea Sonnenmark, 1938.

Hitler Youth force Jews to scrub streets in Vienna, Austria, 1938.

Erika Weihs and her first-grade class, 1924. Erika is second from left in the back row. The girl she later saw being forced to clean streets in Vienna is in the front row, fourth from right.

leave. "I had family and friends there. We had an apartment in the city and a place in the country. We were comfortable. I had a very normal childhood."

But Erika Weihs remembers when the Nazis marched into Vienna: "I heard marching boots everywhere. It seemed everyone had his radio on. I heard Hitler's voice from every window. I saw a girl I knew on her knees, cleaning the street with a brush. A few SS men were standing over her. I remember it because I knew the girl.

"About a month later I was out for a walk. When I came back, Nazis were in our apartment, turning everything upside down. I don't know what they were looking for. They arrested my father and kept him in jail for about six weeks. He was released when he signed over his hardware store to a non-Jew."

Felix Bondi was a young man living in Austria when the Germans marched in. He remembers: "The Nazis asked me and my cousin if we were Jewish. When we said we were, they chased us up and down, up and down, a set of stairs. Then they put us up against the wall and threatened to kill us."

Felix Bondi, 1938.

A Jewish woman being humiliated. The sign she has been forced to wear says that all Jews are swine.

In June 1938 a synagogue in Munich was burned. Two months later the Nuremberg synagogue was set on fire. Several thousand Jews were arrested and put in concentration camps.

In September 1938, just six and a half months after the annexation of Austria, Hitler demanded that the Sudetenland, the German-speaking section of Czechoslovakia, become a part of Germany. In a radio address on Tuesday, September 27, 1938, British Prime Mininster Neville Chamberlain said, "How horrible, how fantastic, how incredible it is that we should be digging trenches and trying on gas masks because of a quarrel in a faraway country between people of whom we know nothing." He then assured the British people that Hitler had told him privately "that once the Sudeten-German incident was settled, that would be the end of German territorial claims in Europe."

Two days later, at the Munich Conference, prime ministers Chamberlain of Britain and Edouard Daladier of France signed the Munich Pact, along with Hitler and Benito Mussolini of Italy. Chamberlain and Daladier gave in to

This Czechoslovakian woman was forced to witness the occupation of the Sudetenland and to salute the German Army.

Hitler's demands in exchange for his promise of peace. The agreement called for Czechoslovakian armed forces to leave the Sudetenland beginning October 1 and for German troops to replace them.

The Czechoslovakian people were not represented at the conference. They felt betrayed. Some threatened to revolt. But Neville Chamberlain returned to England waving the agreement and declared that by appeasing Germany he had brought "peace for our time."

4

"There were flames throughout the city"

Nazi policy wasn't just to harass Jews. It was to force them out of Germany. On the night of Friday, October 28, 1938, thousands of Polish-born Jews were chased out of Germany into Poland. At certain points along the border, Polish guards would not allow the Jews to enter Poland. Many Jews spent a sleepless night at the border in empty railway freight cars, crowded railroad stations, and open fields. Many waited near the border, hoping that an agreement between Polish and German authorities would allow them to return to their homes in Germany. Among the Jews deported to Poland was the Grynszpan family.

Berta Grynszpan sent a postcard to her seventeen-year-old brother Herschel, who was studying in Paris. She wrote that a policeman came to their house at night and told them to take their passports and report to the police station. From there they were taken in a police car to the town hall. They were held there and given orders to leave Germany within four days. "We are penniless," she wrote her brother. "Please send some money to us at Lodz. Love to you from us all, Berta."

Polish Jews being deported, exact location and date unknown.

Herschel became crazed with anger. A few days later, on November 7, 1938, he bought a gun, entered the German embassy in Paris, and shot Ernst vom Rath, a minor German official. The boy told police that he felt that wherever he went he was being chased like an animal. He said, "Being a Jew is not a crime. I am not a dog. I have a right to live and the Jewish people have a right to exist on this earth."

Two days later vom Rath died. That night, on November 9, 1938, following the direction of Minister of Propaganda Joseph Goebbels, who blamed all Jews for the shooting, Nazis and local citizens broke into hundreds of synagogues throughout Germany and Austria. They poured gasoline on the seats and the holy arks and set them on fire. Fire brigades came to protect the nearby buildings, but they did not extinguish the fires in the synagogues.

Vandals broke the windows of thousands of Jewish-owned shops. In some cities huge crowds of Germans and Austrians not involved in the attacks stood by and watched. Jews were forced to watch too as their homes and belongings were destroyed. Many Jews distressed by what was happening committed suicide.

Police kept onlookers from interfering with the vandals. They arrested Jews "for their own protection." And the

Herschel Grynszpan
getting arrested after
shooting Ernst vom Rath.

Jews could not defend themselves. Heinrich Himmler, the
head of German police, issued an order that any Jew found
with a weapon in his possession would be held in a concentration camp for a period of twenty years.

That night in Leipzig a boy was thrown from a third-
story window. Both his legs were broken by the fall. In
Fürth, Jews were dragged to a dark theater and forced to
watch as their friends and family were beaten on stage.

The exact number of Jews killed is not known. Early
Nazi reports were that thirty-six Jews were killed, but the
real number is surely much higher. Thirty thousand Jewish
men were arrested and taken to concentration camps.

A synagogue burns on *Kristallnacht*, November 9, 1938.

Hundreds of synagogues were destroyed. In Germany and Austria, streets where Jews lived and worked were littered with broken windows and debris. That terrible night became known as *Kristallnacht*, the Night of Broken Glass.

A synagogue in Magdeburg, Germany, destroyed on *Kristallnacht*.

Jews were ordered to repair any damage done to their shops and businesses. And insurance companies were ordered not to pay any Jewish claims for damage. Hermann Göring, chief of the German Air Force, was at a meeting just after *Kristallnacht.* He suggested that the Jews be forced to pay a fine of one billion German *Reichsmarks* to atone for the death of vom Rath. His suggestion was approved. Then he added, "I would like to say again, I would not like to be a Jew in Germany."

Julius Rosenzweig lived in Frankfurt am Main. He remembers *Kristallnacht:* "I looked out my window and saw the regular policeman and two Brown Shirts, the SA, come into our building. My mother told me to take a walk. If I didn't, I might have been arrested like so many others. A day or two later I saw Jewish-owned department stores all with broken windows. None of the stores reopened. They had no customers, no merchandise, no security. They were sold to gentiles for almost nothing."

A Jewish store after *Kristallnacht.*

Shulamit Erlebacher with her aunt, 1931.

Manfred Fulda (center front) and his family.

Shulamit Erlebacher lived in Karlsruhe, Germany. She remembers the morning after *Kristallnacht:* "My uncle was the cantor in the great synagogue there. The next morning I came downstairs, and he was sitting there with tears flowing down. 'What's the matter?' I asked. 'They burned my synagogue,' he said. He couldn't stop crying. Then the doorbell rang. It was the SS. 'Where is he? Where is he?' they asked. They took him away to Dachau."

Rabbi Dr. Manfred Fulda remembers *Kristallnacht.* He was nine years old on November 9, 1938. "Our parents were not at home. We four children—my two sisters, my brother and I—were home all alone when our uncle called us and said to turn out the lights, close the shutters, and give the impression that no one was home. We heard the sounds of furniture being thrown out of the windows of the house of our next-door Jewish neighbors. Just at that time we heard a key turn in our own door. The door opened and it was Felix, the seventeen-year-old son of a Catholic family who lived upstairs. When he saw how terribly afraid we were, he told us, 'Don't worry. I'm here now. And I'm not like the rest of them.' Immediately he changed into his Hitler Youth uniform, looked out a second-floor window, and shouted to the Nazi mob, 'This house has been sold to Aryans. Any damage you will do, you will be responsible for. There are no more Jews here.' The mob moved on, and so we were saved by this young man who proved with his heroic courage that he really was different from all the rest of them."

Cantor Moshe Ehrlich remembers *Kristallnacht* in Vienna: "We lived across from a school, which was made into a prison. We heard terrible screams of people being beaten. People threw themselves out of windows. There were flames throughout the city."

Cantor Ehrlich also remembers that the destruction and the beatings didn't end after *Kristallnacht:* "The fear was constant. We had the same fear a week later and a month later. Whatever wasn't destroyed then was destroyed later."

Thea Sonnenmark lived in Vienna. She remembers *Kristallnacht:* "I belonged to a Zionist group. That night I was coming home from a meeting with a friend of mine. We saw flames coming out from buildings, and uniformed Nazis breaking windows with rocks and axes. Some SA started to chase us. We ran into a building, closed and locked the door, and waited. When we were sure they would be gone, we came out. But they were still there. They chased us some more, until they caught us. They let me go, but they sent my friend to Dachau. We heard from him once, about two weeks later, but never again. I assume he died at Dachau."

Fred Erlebacher was arrested on *Kristallnacht.* He remembers: "They came to my store and told me to go to city hall. When I got there, I saw every Jewish man from the village. It was a cold November night, but some of them were still in their pajamas. There was an American citizen, a tourist. He said, 'I'm an American citizen.' They said, 'You're a Jew,' and kicked him hard. The SS took us for a march of a couple of hours through the town, and the town residents looked at us as if we were criminals. They marched us to the next town and put us in a barn. The next morning they marched us to the railway station. They loaded us into a freight train and took us to Dachau. When we got there, they opened the doors. 'Out!' they yelled at us, and knocked us with the butts of their guns. I was in Dachau for five weeks. My mother brought papers saying that I would leave Germany, so I was released. At that

Jewish men are marched through the streets of Baden-Baden, after *Kristallnacht*.

Louis Fulda, father of Manfred Fulda, 1936.

time it was enough if you just left Germany."

Rabbi Dr. Manfred Fulda's father was arrested in Frankfurt am Main on the day after *Kristallnacht* and sent to the Buchenwald concentration camp. He remembers: "My mother had finally gotten a visa for him, and he was released after several weeks. He had lost eighty pounds. The Nazis had shaved off his entire beard. He had been severely beaten, and he was covered all over with bloody wounds. When I saw him lying on the couch in our living room, I turned to my mother and asked her, 'Who is that man?' I just did not recognize him. 'It's your own father,' she answered me."

Many people throughout the world were shocked and saddened by the events of *Kristallnacht*. There were protests and front-page stories in just about every American newspaper, as well as numerous editorials condemning Germany. The Nazis answered the protests with a warning that any actions against Germany would lead to more Jewish suffering.

At a press conference a few days later, President Franklin D. Roosevelt of the United States said, "The news of the past few days from Germany has deeply shocked public opinion in the United States. Such news from any part of the world would inevitably produce a similar profound reaction among Americans in every part of the nation. I myself could scarcely believe that such things could occur in a twentieth-century civilization." In protest the United States ambassador to Germany was told to return to Washington.

In 1933 there were about seven hundred thousand Jews living in Germany and Austria. But every year, as Nazi policy became increasingly anti-Jewish, thousands of Jews left. The horrors of *Kristallnacht* made the need to escape even more urgent.

Anita Federman lived in Liverpool, England. She remembers: "Sometime before World War Two began, Helga, a Jewish girl my age, came from Germany to live with us. Her parents couldn't get out, but she did. There were lots of kids like her, and many of them had emotional problems. Imagine, they were torn from their families and were sent to a foreign-speaking country! The Jewish organization which brought her to us and looked after these children tried desperately to keep in touch with their families. But for the year Helga was with us, she never heard from her parents. It was a difficult time."

Anita Federman, 1945.

For many Jews trying to leave Germany and Austria, there was no place to go. Guards of bordering countries turned them back. At the same press conference at which President Roosevelt decried *Kristallnacht*, he was asked if any place had been found for the Jews who wished to leave Germany. He replied, "No, the time is not ripe for that." When he was asked if he would propose a loosening of immigration laws to allow more Jewish refugees to come to the United States, he said he would not.

U.S. Private First Class
Arthur Federman, 1943.

Jews in the United States held rallies, signed petitions, and sent letters to President Roosevelt, but polls conducted at the time found that most Americans were against letting Jewish refugees into the United States, even refugee children. And the U.S. government refused to open its gates to the Jews.

Arthur Federman was a young boy living in the United States when the Nazis rose to power. He didn't hear too much about the rise of anti-Semitism in Germany, only what his father read to him from the Yiddish newspapers at the dinner table. It all seemed so far away, until 1938. "I went with my father to a rally at Madison Square Garden. There was a huge crowd. People who could not get into the Garden were standing in the streets. There were speeches and loud reactions from the audience, calling for action. People were disillusioned with President Roosevelt because nothing was being done. I left that rally very anxious about the trouble in Germany."

In July 1938, at Evian, France, delegates from thirty-two countries met to discuss the problem of Jewish refugees. But delegates complained of unemployment and overpopulation in their countries. Large, underpopulated countries with no unemployment problems didn't want Jews either. Some delegates said their countries could accept only agricultural workers, and Jews, denied the right to own land for hundreds of years in Europe, were not farmers. No place was found for the huge number of Jews desperate to escape Nazi persecution.

Some Jews tried to escape to Switzerland. Although Switzerland bordered Germany and other countries either allied with Germany or occupied by it, it remained neutral throughout the war. Clara Wachter Feldman remembers: "As a young girl I made it into Switzerland. I was pulled out of a creek by Swiss soldiers and brought to a military barracks. For five days and nights I sat on dirty straw. I was interrogated by a Swiss officer. He told me, 'We're handing you over to the Germans. They know what to do with Jews.' " But the Swiss didn't act on their threat. They didn't return her to Germany.

Edith Rhein remembers: "The day after the Nazis marched into Austria, my father left. He had a German passport, so he was able to travel. But on the train with him were Jews with Austrian passports. They were not allowed to leave the country. My father told us often that he would never forget their cries and screams."

Cantor Moshe Ehrlich was in Vienna. He remembers: "My father wanted to get out. No one would take us. The only nearby country not under Hitler was Switzerland. My dad smuggled himself into Switzerland. They sent him back. Later he did get in. We got visas to come to America, but the American consul made my father return to Vienna to have his visa stamped. This was at the height of German atrocities, and they, the Americans, sent him back."

The British controlled Palestine, and it was almost completely closed to Jews. Many of the Jews who escaped to Palestine by boat were considered by the British to be illegal immigrants, and sent back to Europe.

In 1939 a plan was proposed by a U.S. senator and a congresswoman to save twenty thousand Jewish children under the age of fourteen by bringing them to the United States. It was supported by former President Hoover and by Eleanor Roosevelt, the President's wife. But not by the President. It never passed through Congress.

In 1939 the *St. Louis*, a ship with more than nine hundred Jewish refugees on board, was turned away by Cuba even though all the passengers had landing certificates. As it

Jews aboard the *St. Louis* before it was turned away from Cuba.

began its trip back to Europe, the ship passed very close to the shores of Florida. The U.S. Coast Guard followed the ship. The Coast Guard had instructions from the government to make sure that not one refugee jumped off the

St. Louis and swam ashore. On their return to Europe most of the refugees were let into Holland, Belgium, France, and England. These countries were still free. The refugees felt safe, but most would not survive the Holocaust. Within a year Holland, Belgium, and France were conquered by the German Army and subjected to Nazi rule.

Other Jews tried to escape Nazi persecution by boat. Among the many who suffered were the 769 Romanian passengers on the *S.S. Struma*. It was a broken-down cattle boat headed for Palestine. The Jews boarded it in Costanta, Romania, on December 12, 1941. Four days later the boat broke down near the port of Istanbul, Turkey. The passengers were not allowed ashore, and British authorities refused to grant them permission to enter Palestine. The ship didn't move for more than two months. The passengers displayed a large sign, "Save Us!" but no one did. On February 23, 1942, the ship was tied to a tugboat and pulled into the Black Sea. In the middle of the sea the *S.S. Struma* was unhooked from the tug. The next morning it sank in the icy water. Only one passenger survived. Seven hundred and sixty-eight others, including seventy children, drowned. It was reported many years later that the broken-down cattle boat was sunk by a Soviet submarine.

5

"A date which will
live in infamy"

Hitler's war of conquest did not end when he united Europe's German-speaking peoples. On September 1, 1939, his troops invaded Poland.

German dive-bombers attacked the Polish Air Force, hit-

German soldiers boarding a train to Poland. The handwritten sign says, "We are going to Poland to beat up Jews."

ting most of the Polish airplanes while they were still on the ground. Then German tanks and armored cars rolled in, followed by foot soldiers. There was little the Polish Army could do to stop this German *Blitzkrieg*, this "lightning war." On September 17 the Soviets, who were then allies of the Germans, attacked Poland from the east, and before the end of September, Poland fell.

Alfred Lipson remembers when the German Army invaded Radom, Poland: "Early that morning, at six o'clock, several German airplanes bombed primarily the airfield and the Jewish quarter. The first victims of the war in Radom were Jewish civilians."

On Sunday, September 3, 1939, two days after the invasion of Poland, at 11:00 A.M., Britain declared war on Germany. France declared itself at war with Germany later the same day, at 5:00 P.M. The Second World War had begun.

Many people alive in Europe in 1939 remembered the war that had begun just twenty-five years earlier, the Great War, a war that had been called "the war to end all wars." It didn't. Beginning in September 1939, people blackened their windows to protect against nighttime enemy attacks. In Britain preparations were made to distribute gas masks to the entire population, including Mickey Mouse gas masks for the children. Air-raid sirens were tested. Air-raid shelters were built. Posters appeared everywhere, instructing people how to protect themselves during an attack. Within the first few days of September, more than three million small children, women, old men, and invalids were evacuated from the larger cities in England. They went to less populated areas, away from the danger of attack by German bombers.

In April 1940 the Germans invaded Denmark and Nor-

Alfred Lipson.

way. Within one day Denmark was defeated. Two months later, even with the help of Britain and France, Norway fell too.

While the fighting was still going on in Norway, the Germans attacked Luxembourg, Holland, and Belgium.

Luxembourg had only a small army. It fell in one day. Holland fell four days later. And after eighteen days of fighting, King Leopold of Belgium surrendered to the Germans.

The Germans attacked France in May 1940. German armored divisions won battle after battle. French, British, and Belgian soldiers retreated to the beach at Dunkirk, a seaport in northern France. More than three hundred thousand soldiers escaped to England in steamers, speedboats, rowboats, just about anything that could float. It was a remarkable rescue. But France was lost.

This was Hitler's sweetest victory. Almost twenty-two years earlier Hitler had been in a hospital bed when Ger-

German soldiers marching into France.

many had agreed to unfavorable terms with France. Now he took from a museum in Paris the same railroad car in which Germany had agreed to the terms that ended the First World War. It was brought to the exact spot in the French forest where it had been in 1918. And there the French surrendered to Hitler.

Germany had many enemies, but there were also nations that joined forces with her. Benito Mussolini of Italy signed an agreement with Hitler in October 1936. Each country would support the other's foreign policies, forming what became known as the Rome-Berlin Axis. From then on Germany and her military partners were known as the Axis Powers. When Japan joined the Axis in September 1940, it became known as the Rome-Berlin-Tokyo Axis. Several smaller countries joined the Axis too, including Hungary, Romania, and Bulgaria. The many nations at war with the Axis, including Britain, France, Canada, and later the Soviet Union and the United States, were known as the Allies.

In April 1941 the German blitzkrieg, with more than a thousand planes and more than a million soldiers, invaded Greece and Yugoslavia. They fell too. And as country after country fell to the German Army, the Jews who lived in those countries fell into Nazi hands.

Hitler dances a jig as France surrenders.

Early on the morning of December 7, 1941, 350 Japanese bombers attacked American ships, airplanes, and soldiers at Pearl Harbor, Hawaii. The next day President Roosevelt told Congress, "Yesterday, December 7, 1941— a date which will live in infamy—the United States of America was suddenly and deliberately attacked by naval and air forces of the Empire of Japan." The United States declared war on Japan, and three days later, on December 11, Hitler called Roosevelt a "madman" and declared war

The Japanese attack on
Pearl Harbor, Hawaii,
December 7, 1941.

on the United States. Before the war would end, more than
fifty countries would be involved, most of them joining the
Allies and fighting against the Axis countries. The world
was at war.

6

" 'Throw down a piece of bread. Give us a piece of bread' "

In 1939, when the Germans marched into Poland, there were more than three million Jews living there. They were mostly poor, but Jewish culture and religious life in Poland were strong. There were many Jewish schools, synagogues, theaters, and newspapers.

A Jewish library in Vilna, Poland, 1920s.

A *melamed* (teacher of Jewish subjects) with his students, Warsaw, 1938.

Carl Hamada and his brothers in Poland, 1933. Carl is at right.

Carl Hamada remembers living as a child in Frysztak, Poland: "There was a flourishing Jewish life in the small Polish towns. Ours was mostly Jewish, and every Jew there was Orthodox. It was a close community, and very poor. People worked in small stores or went to other towns and sold there on market day. On Jewish holidays our town closed up."

The SS followed the German Army into Poland. They subjected Jews to the many Nazi anti-Jewish regulations. And on October 24, 1939, the SS in Wloclawek, a city in central Poland with about ten thousand Jews, added a new decree. Every Jew was to wear a large yellow triangle on his or her clothing. The SS in other areas followed the example of Wloclawek and ordered Jews to wear distinctive badges. Among the badges the Jews were forced to wear in different areas were Stars of David, white armbands with a Star of David sewn on, yellow armbands, and round yellow patches.

Beginning on September 1, 1941, the Jews in Germany

were required to wear yellow Stars of David with the word *Jude* printed in the center. Inge Auerbacher lived in Jebenhausen, Germany. She was just six years old in 1941. She remembers: "I was so little, and the star seemed so big. I didn't feel shame, but I was scared when I wore it. We were branded. It was like we wore a large yellow neon sign pointing to us as Jews."

Jewish life in Poland changed drastically under Nazi control. Carol Frenkel Lipson remembers the winter of 1939–40 in Radom, Poland: "The German occupiers set up district offices to govern Poland, and the people working there needed a place to live. We were assigned a civilian from Berlin, Herr Maier and his wife. We gave them two rooms and we were happy to do it, because it enabled us to stay in our apartment. The winter was very cold, and we had hoped that perhaps we could benefit from Maier's coal allotment.

"Something funny happened then, although we didn't think at the time that it was funny. The Germans had posted all sorts of public notices on walls and kiosks all over Radom prohibiting Jews from using the sidewalks, or that men had to take off their hats every time they passed a German. One of the decrees was that Jews were not allowed to own a radio under the penalty of death. We had to stand in line to turn in our radios at a German depot. Well, my sister Pauline had a beautiful voice, and one evening we asked her to sing for us. All of a sudden the door to our room was thrown open. 'Who is hiding a radio here?' Herr Maier yelled. We were stunned. Perhaps it was a provocation. Perhaps he hid a radio somewhere, we thought, so he could report us to the police, have us shot, and then take over the entire apartment. My father stood up and told him categorically that we had no radio. 'But,' Maier said, 'I have

Nazis forced Jews to sew identifying stars on their clothes. These Jews are from Romania.

Carol Frenkel Lipson, 1939.

53

just heard Erna Sack's voice!' That was a famous German soprano, the most popular singer in Europe at the time. 'No, it was our Pauline,' we told him. He didn't believe us until she sang for him. Following this incident, he would invite his coworkers to our apartment to hear Pauline sing.

"Later, while in Auschwitz, my sister was often summoned to the block supervisor's room to sing, thus earning some extra soup and bread, which she shared with me."

Alfred Lipson remembers when the Germans entered Radom: "They made announcements. Jews were not permitted to hold any meetings, to hold religious services. The synagogue was turned into a stable. Jews met privately to hold Rosh Hashanah and Yom Kippur services. The Germans would have never known about this. They didn't have the manpower to go from house to house. But our Polish neighbors pointed out where services were being held. The Germans raided the homes on Yom Kippur, and with their *talesim* [prayer shawls] still on, they forced the men to dig ditches to make latrines.

"One of the people they forced to work that day was an old *melamed* [Jewish teacher]. The SS pushed pork into his mouth. The *melamed* spit it out. They kept pushing it in, and he kept spitting it out and fighting them. Another SS man took pictures of how they forced a Jew to eat pork on Yom Kippur. Finally the Germans lost patience and shot him and then put the pork sausage in his mouth. He died there, in my presence."

Carol Frenkel Lipson remembers: "The SS was familiar with the Jewish calendar. Every holiday was observed by the SS with another action." Her husband, Alfred Lipson, remembers Purim, 1943, in Radom: "There were rumors that the Germans were negotiating with the Allies for an

A Jew in Lublin, Poland, is forced to wear a large Jewish star broken off the gates of a synagogue.

exchange of Jews for German prisoners of war. Then the SS issued an order for a list of professionals and other college graduates. People fought to get on the list, until almost two hundred had signed up. They dressed in their best clothes, said good-bye to all of us, and then went to the trucks which were waiting. But we all saw the trucks didn't take them to the railroad station. They drove to the cemetery. Dr. Anatol Fried wrestled a rifle away from an SS man and knocked him to the ground. Dr. Fried was shot in the head. An attorney, Wladek Weisfuss, and many others fought bravely. They were all killed. Some escaped by hiding under the truck. But one hundred and fifty men, women, and children were murdered. The joyous holiday of Purim had ended in tragedy."

The Nazi plan was to gather the Jews from small towns

Nazi soldiers guarding an entrance to a ghetto. The sign says, "Living area for Jews. Entrance is prohibited."

and villages into central locations—larger cities near railroad lines. Throughout Poland and the rest of Nazi-controlled Europe, Jews were forced to leave their homes, taking along only as much as they could carry, and move into ghettos, walled-in sections of the cities. The possessions they left behind, their furniture, clothing, homes and businesses, became Nazi property.

By 1944 Arthur Rubin's father had already been taken to a labor camp. He remembers the day his mother, five brothers, and one sister were taken from their home in Hungary: "Early one morning we saw policemen standing in front of our gate, and we were told we could not leave our home. Shortly after that we were given three hours to pack. We could take along only what we could wear and carry by hand. Now how do you pack for a trip for eight people when you don't know where you are going, how long you will be away, and what you will be doing? All of us put on extra clothes, like two shirts, two pairs of pants, and our best shoes. To this day, more than forty years later, at times I wake up trembling. I remember being told to leave my home, being robbed of every bit of security I felt. As hard as I try, I cannot describe this feeling."

Ernest Honig remembers when the Germans marched into Munkacs, Hungary: "They gave an order for Jews to assemble at a certain spot on Saturday. A ghetto was to be set up, and we were to build a fence enclosing the area. But most Jews would not work on the Sabbath, and few people showed up. There was a house-to-house search—how well I remember! My father, a religious man who never worked on Saturday, was at home when the Germans came. They ordered him to say a prayer and then machine-gunned him to death. He was the first person to be killed by the Germans in my hometown. I heard the shots."

Hirsh Altusky remembers when the Warsaw ghetto was

Hirsh Altusky, 1930.

Boys in the Warsaw ghetto.

established: "We interpreted everything for good. When Jews were first forced to build walls to close in the ghetto, we thought they were for defense, to stop the Russians if the Germans had to retreat. Every day there were rumors that the border would be moved up to the Vistula River, that the Russians were coming. Every two or three days someone would come and say that he saw the Russians coming. That was our hope."

The ghettos were terribly crowded. Each apartment was shared by many families. Each room was shared by six to seven people. Thousands more lived in the streets. There was very little food in the ghettos. Children searched the streets, the garbage, for something to eat. Jews died of disease. They died of hunger. Ghetto gates were guarded. There were many restrictions on when Jews could enter or leave. Jews caught outside the ghetto were killed. Inside the ghettos the Nazis assigned Jewish community leaders to be members of the internal ghetto government, the *Judenrat*. They were responsible for seeing that Nazi orders were carried out.

A woman lying dead of starvation in a Warsaw ghetto street.

Despite the overcrowding, the hunger, and the many Nazi restrictions in the ghettos, Jews tried to maintain some semblance of normal life. Alfred Lipson remembers: "All schools in the Radom ghetto were closed. One day my two younger sisters, Myra and Dina, who were twelve and fourteen, asked me to teach them. They were very upset not to be getting an education. I agreed. We found an isolated place in our apartment, and I taught them algebra, Latin, and Hebrew, my favorite subjects. Teaching in the Radom ghetto was against Nazi regulations. We could have been killed. In order to avoid any surprise visit by German police, my brother Sam, who was sixteen at the time, stood guard.

"After a while my sisters asked if they could bring some friends along. The class grew to five and then to nine children. They wanted me to give them homework, and when I gave it to them, it wasn't enough. They wanted more.

"I remember thinking about the futility of it all, about the tragic uselessness of teaching Latin and algebra under those circumstances. But then I would see the enthusiasm of my sisters and her friends, and I felt good resisting Nazi orders."

The ghetto in Lodz, Poland, was set up in the poorest section of the city in the winter of 1940. Many of the small one- and two-room apartments had no running water. Toilets were outside. The ghetto was surrounded by barbed-wire fence and guarded by Nazi police.

Ruth Bestman lived for a time in the Lodz ghetto. She remembers: "The ghettos were the worst for me. You were with your family, and you saw them dying. We moved into a room that was used to make coffins. Of the three families who lived there, I was the only one to survive."

Hirsh Altusky lived in the Warsaw ghetto. He remembers: "There were two sections, a big ghetto and a small ghetto. To go from one part to the other was a bridge. Jews *benched gomel* [said a prayer of thanks] when they came safely off that bridge, because you were at the Germans' mercy. One day they hit you if you didn't tip your hat to them. The next day they hit you if you did. 'How dare a Jew tip his hat to greet a German!' "

Erwin Baum lived in the Warsaw ghetto too. He remembers: "There was no food, no clothes, just pure hunger and starvation."

Ruth Bestman (at right), with another patient in a sanatorium, recovering from the tuberculosis she contracted in the Lodz ghetto and in Auschwitz. This photograph was taken in 1945, after liberation.

A Jewish man looking out
of the ghetto in Lodz,
Poland.

A child eats in the street in
the Lodz ghetto.

Jews stood in the streets and tried to trade whatever
they still had—clothing, books, pots—for some bread.
Hirsh Altusky remembers: "At night children were crying
and begging, 'Throw down a piece of bread. Give us a piece
of bread.' Every day when you walked out of the house,
you saw dead bodies, skin and bones covered with newspaper."

Erwin Baum remembers: "Children died in the streets.

" 'Give us a piece of bread' "

Every morning I climbed over the wall. I bent down and waited for a car to pass, and then I ran alongside it. I went to the market. There were all kinds of goodies there—food and bread. I bought as many loaves of bread as I could carry. One day a Polish policeman caught me with the bread, and with his club he beat me over the head, over my body, over my hands, and he took all the bread from me, all six loaves."

Jews were afraid to challenge Nazi authority. Hirsh Altusky remembers: "A Polish police officer caught a Jew who was in some sort of trouble. The Jew injured the policeman, and that night they took all the men from Nine Nalewki Street, fifty-one men. No one knew for quite a few days what happened to them. But then the *Judenrat* was notified to pick up the bodies and was told to pay for the bullets the Nazis used to kill the men."

A brother and sister share their small ration of food in the Lodz ghetto.

Children lying in the street in the Lodz ghetto.

7

"We didn't know what was happening to us"

By the middle of 1941 as many as twenty thousand European Jews had starved to death in the ghettos. Ten thousand more had been murdered. But for the Nazis the Jews weren't dying quickly enough. In June 1941, with the invasion of the Soviet Union, the Nazi program of mass killing began.

Einsatzgruppen, Nazi murder squads, followed the German Army into the Soviet Union. They ordered the Jews to gather for "resettlement." Then the Nazis took their valuables and forced them to march to barren areas, dig, undress, and wait. Parents and grandparents waited with their children. The victims did not know what was about to happen until they saw the Nazis raise their machine guns and fire. Many fell into the holes they had just finished digging. Some were only wounded, but most were killed. With shovels and bulldozers, the dirt was pushed back into the holes. The Nazis buried them all, the living and the dead.

Paul Blobel was a member of the SS. After the war, at Nuremberg, he described the actions of the *Einsatzgrup-*

A Polish Jew is forced to dig his own grave before being shot.

pen in the Ukraine in September 1941. He said that he was, at times, assigned to execute "undesirables." And he described their execution: "One of my leaders who was in charge of this execution squad gave the order to shoot. Since they were kneeling on the brink of the mass grave, the victims fell, as a rule, at once into the mass grave."

In October 1942, Hermann Graebe, an engineer in the Ukraine section of Russia, heard rifle shots coming from behind a large mound of dirt. This is part of a statement he made and signed that was read after the war at the trials of Nazi war criminals in Nuremberg: "I walked around the mound and found myself confronted by a tremendous grave. People were closely wedged together and lying on top of each other so that only their heads were visible. Nearly all had blood running over their shoulders from their heads. Some of the people were still moving. Some were lifting their arms and turning their heads to show that they were still alive. The pit was already two-thirds full. I estimated that it contained about a thousand people. I looked for the man who did the shooting. He was an SS man, who sat at the edge of the narrow end of the pit, his feet dangling into the pit. He had a tommy gun on his knees and was smoking a cigarette."

In Chelmno, Poland, many thousands of Jews were locked into trucks, which were sealed shut. The trucks were filled with exhaust smoke as they drove toward the open pits. By the time they arrived, the Jews were dead. Their bodies were dropped into the pits and covered with dirt.

The Nazis killed others, too. In the European countries they conquered, the Nazis killed millions of innocent men, women, and children. They killed more than two hundred thousand Gypsies. Thousands of homosexuals were killed. Thousands of people suffering from mental illness were killed too. And more than two million Soviet prisoners of war who had laid down their guns were either deprived of food and starved to death or shot.

According to Nazi plans, the Russians, Poles, Czechs, and other conquered peoples who were allowed to live were to become slaves of the German nation. But there were no such plans for Jews. The Nazis planned to kill every Jew in Europe.

The Nazis were killing Jews in huge numbers, but it wasn't until January 20, 1942, that they devised their "Final Solution" to the Jewish problem. That day sixteen Nazi leaders met just outside Berlin, at Wannsee. According to their notes at the meeting, "Europe is to be combed through from West to East in the course of the practical implementation of the final solution. . . . The evacuated Jews will be taken, group by group, to the so-called transit ghettos, in order to be transported further east from there." Their "Final Solution" was the planned destruction of all eleven million Jews in the countries Germany already controlled and the ones they expected to conquer.

Jews in the ghettos were told they were being taken to labor camps or just that they were being "resettled" farther east. Many were already starving, too sick, too weak, even to question what was happening. Their organizations had been broken up long ago. They were mostly cut off from people outside their ghettos. The Jews were herded into freight trains—cattle cars bound for camps in Auschwitz-Birkenau, Maidanek, Treblinka, Dachau, Buchenwald, Sobibor, Chelmno, Belzec, Bergen-Belsen, and others. Some had heard rumors about these camps. But who could believe such gruesome stories?

Ernest Honig remembers: "We couldn't wait to get on the next train, so we could get jobs, so we could meet our families."

Judy Schonfeld Schabes was fifteen when the train took her from Beregszasz, Hungary, to Auschwitz. She remembers: "One day cattle cars arrived. We didn't know what was happening to us. That's for sure. My family and I were in the first group taken from the ghetto."

Leo Machtingier lived in Kielce, Poland. At four thirty one morning he was told to get up and get out, or he would be shot. As Jews ran to the square, the Germans separated those with jobs from the others. Leo Machtingier was lucky to have a job and was one of those spared. After the roundup he walked back through the town. "There were so many dead. They forced some of us to dig a big grave and drop the dead in. There were five hundred, maybe six hundred, laid out like herring."

Alfred Lipson was in a ghetto in Radom, Poland. In August 1942 many of the Jews there were deported. Alfred Lipson was spared. He remembers: "A few days later a young man came back. He had found a hiding place after the train had stopped at Treblinka. He hid under the train,

Judy Schonfeld Schabes wearing her school cap, Hungary, 1942.

Leo Machtingier, 1946.

65

Leo Fischelberg, 1942.
This photograph was taken
in the Bochnia ghetto.

by the wheels. He grabbed my coat by the lapels, and with a frightened look in his eyes he said, 'I was there. I was there. They were all gassed.' I wouldn't listen. I interrupted him several times. I tried to get away from him. What he was telling me was completely unbelievable. It couldn't penetrate my mind. The man ran to other people. We didn't want to listen."

In 1942 Leo Fischelberg was in the Bochnia ghetto in the Krakow district of Poland. He was just twelve years old. From a hideout he shared with many others, he witnessed a roundup of children. "First they took the older children and then the younger ones. I saw mothers holding onto their children's clothing and begging, begging the Nazis, 'Please, please, don't take my child.' By the time the children were loaded into open trucks, the mothers were exhausted from crying. Then, while everyone watched, one of the Nazis took a machine gun and shot a few of the grieving mothers."

Hirsh Altusky (lower right)
with his family, 1930.

Mendy Berger and his family, 1937. Mendy is in the back row, on the right.

Hirsh Altusky remembers: "Our transport was sent to Maidanek, and I was separated from my father. When I tried to join him, the Nazis said, 'You don't need your father. We are your father now.' "

Mendy Berger was seventeen years old when he was taken from Munkacs, Hungary. He remembers going to the train that took him to Auschwitz: "We were chased from the ghetto to the train station. As we ran, and some of us were killed, the Christian people of the community were watching as if it was a parade, applauding, laughing. One man whom my father and uncle had helped many times smiled and yelled at us in Hungarian, '*Shoha vissa*—You will never return.' "

And he remembers the train ride: "One hundred people standing in a locked railroad car, no food, no water, people dying, the smell of the dead, and we had no toilets. We did it right where we were standing, and we couldn't move away from it."

Arthur Rubin and his family were in a ghetto for just ten days. Then they were taken by train, in cattle cars, to Auschwitz. "The thirst on that trip was unbearable. Chil-

Railroad tracks approaching Sobibor death camp.

dren were crying for water, and mothers' hearts were torn because they were unable to help them. I remember traveling through Poland. The train stopped at various stations. There were women standing near the railroad tracks with buckets of water, and they would hand us cups of water through the small opening in exchange for something like a shirt or blouse. When we had nothing left to exchange, they spitefully spilled the water on the ground. I remember this very clearly."

Hirsh Altusky was on a train destined for Maidanek. He remembers: "It was hot. Everyone was thirsty. When the train was stopped at a siding, Polish train workers traded us something to drink. They wanted gold, watches, anything. They wanted big money. I gave five hundred zlotys for a little flask of vodka which cost maybe one zloty. I drank the vodka, and I slept, drunk, until we came to Maidanek."

"We didn't know what was happening to us"

Ruth Bestman was taken by train from the Lodz ghetto to Auschwitz. She remembers: "There was yelling, crying, and screaming in the train, so many people, one on top of the other, just pushed in. When the doors opened and we saw the Germans, they seemed like giants. They yelled at us to get out and leave all our belongings on the train. Then they separated the men from the women. I was with my older sister and her husband. He went one way, we went the other way. We never saw him again. He was in his twenties and already quite an important person. He was killed in Auschwitz."

Cecilia Bernstein was a teenager when she left Munkacs, Hungary. She remembers: "We came to Auschwitz on the railroad. It was so crowded, we took off our shoes so we wouldn't step on someone. We had no food. My brother Ari fainted from hunger. My mother cried, 'Ari is dying in my hands!' " But he wasn't quite dead. He would die later in Auschwitz.

Jews as they arrive at the camp at Auschwitz.

Leo Fischelberg remembers: "In Bergen-Belsen my job was to take out the ones who died on the trains. We carried them by their legs and arms and had to throw them onto a wagon, then bring them to an open pit and drop them in. I did this for five months. I was fifteen. . . . We once tried to take someone not completely dead and put him on top of the wagon so he could breathe. The Nazis beat us. We wanted to save a life, and they yelled at us, '*Schnell! Schnell! Macht los!*—Quick! Quick! Get going!' To them, to save a life was a waste of time."

Ernest Honig remembers when he arrived at Auschwitz: "We saw huge chimneys, and smoke, and there was a terrible smell. My brother and I were standing next to each other. We wondered what that could be. One of us said, 'Maybe a factory. Maybe they're making rubber. Maybe that's where we'll be working.' But it occurred to me, as it must have to my brother, that maybe they were burning people."

Jewish prisoners in a train on their way to one of the death camps.

70

"We didn't know what was happening to us"

When Arthur Rubin arrived at Auschwitz, he saw the chimneys too. "We thought maybe it was a bakery. Who could imagine they were doing these things to people?" He remembers when the doors of the cattle car he was riding in were opened: "Strong-looking inmates with shaved heads were screaming at us, ' *'Raus! 'Raus!*—Out! Out!' We were told to line up, the males in one row and the females and little children in another row. Then we were moved forward. We approached a man with one foot up, resting on a chair. He would just say 'Right' or 'Left.' Once in a while he would ask a question. It was all done very fast."

Lee Potasinski, 1941.

Lee Potasinski remembers when he arrived at Auschwitz. "An old man was next to me on the train. 'I think we're all finished,' he said. Then he said the *kaddish* [the Jewish prayer said in memory of the dead]. 'Why are you saying that?' I asked. He told me, 'I'm saying it for myself.' "

Soon after Arthur Rubin arrived at Auschwitz, he was asked to sign a postcard. "They were so deceitful. The card said, 'I arrived well and in good health. I am doing well. Regards and kisses to you.' This was before we knew what was really happening in the camp. They wanted us to write, so people back home would be willing to come too, and they hoped we would give them an address of someone who was hiding from them."

Esther Klein remembers when she was taken to work each morning in Dachau: "SS men were with us. If we didn't walk fast enough, we were beaten. As we walked through the camp, we passed wagons piled high with the dead. But some of them were still alive, and we heard weak cries: 'Water. Water. Help me. Help me.' "

The camps were enclosed by high, electrified-barbed-wire fences. There were watchtowers with searchlights and

71

Auschwitz.

guards holding machine guns. SS guards patroled the camps. There was no way out.

Two young Jews escaped Auschwitz-Birkenau on April 7, 1944, and reached the Jewish underground in Slovakia, part of Czechoslovakia. They described what faced a prisoner who tried to escape. "If at the roll call any prisoner is found missing, an alarm is sounded. . . . The guards of the outer fence remain in their towers, and the guards of the inner fence also take up their posts. Hundreds of SS men with bloodhounds search the area between the two fences. The sirens alert the whole region so that even after miraculously breaking through the two guarded fences, the escaping prisoner faces the danger of falling into the hands of numerous German police and SS patrols. . . . During our

two years of imprisonment, many attempted to escape, but with the exception of two or three, all were brought back dead or alive."

At the camps the Jews were divided. First the men were separated from the women. Then those who were chosen to work as slave laborers were sent to one side, those who were to be killed to the other.

Alfred Lipson remembers Dr. Josef Mengele, the Nazi official who did the selection at Auschwitz: "He was a tall, handsome man, impeccably dressed, with a smile on his face. He tried to look charming. It gave us a sense of security."

Lena Mandelbaum remembers: "I was sent to the right, with my sister. My mother and my two brothers, my aunt,

High-tension wires surrounding the camp at Auschwitz.

Selection at Auschwitz.

uncles, and grandparents were sent to the left. We never saw them again." They were killed in Auschwitz.

It was usually the young and strong who were selected for work. The old, the weak, and the very young were immediately killed.

Ruth Bestman remembers walking with a group of prisoners in Auschwitz. Among them was a woman with her two daughters. "One said 'Mother' in Polish. The Germans heard that and knew the woman was much older than the rest of us. They took her right out to the gas chambers. Most of us had already lost our parents, but here was a mother with her daughters. There was crying. It's still clear in my memory. One of the sisters committed suicide later in Israel. Maybe she felt guilty because this is how her mother perished."

"We didn't know what was happening to us"

Judy Schonfeld Schabes was selected for work. But for six weeks, until she was taken to Cologne, Germany, to clear rubble from the streets after Allied bombings, she was in Auschwitz. She remembers the barracks: "We slept eight people on one shelf. There was some straw scattered on the shelf and one blanket for all of us. We had no idea of days or dates. We weren't aware of anything. We were so scared, so intimidated, we didn't even know what was happening on the next shelf. In the middle of the night one of the older prisoners would sing, 'Get up. Get up. Get dressed. Get dressed. You are not at home. You are with Hitler in camp.' We would have to march outside and stand

Women prisoners in the barracks at Auschwitz.

Esther Himmelfarb
Peterseil, 1946.

in rows so they could count us. I wondered why they counted us. Where did they expect us to go?"

Ruth Bestman remembers the day she arrived in Auschwitz: "We were stripped of everything and shaved. The only thing I was holding was a photograph of my parents, which of course I had to give up. When we went in for a shower, we were told to leave our clothes. We were taken out a different way and thrown a dress, no underwear."

Esther Himmelfarb Peterseil remembers when she arrived at Auschwitz: "They took us through the gate. There was music. We left all our belongings. They stripped us. By this time I didn't know where my mother was. They took us to the showers. They shaved us. After that I wouldn't recognize my own sister."

Carol Frenkel Lipson remembers how she felt during the three months she was at Auschwitz: "We had to undress in front of thousands of people. I remember being ashamed, embarrassed, and at the same time frightened and worried. There were beautiful women, but when their heads were shaved, they looked ugly. This was one way our oppressors found to dehumanize and degrade all of us, especially women. They gave us a rag of a dress and no underwear. It was unbearable for us women to stand for hours in the wind and cold—and I can tell you that Auschwitz had terrible weather. We could go to the 'toilet' only at prescribed times, twice a day, and in a great hurry. Imagine rows of women sitting in public over a hole in the ground. For anyone who had come from reasonably human circumstances, the daily routine in Auschwitz had a dehumanizing effect at every step."

Carol Frenkel Lipson remembers when the number A-24742 was tattooed on her arm: "We were worried when we weren't given numbers right away. We knew if we didn't get a number, we were destined for the crematorium. In Auschwitz a number meant life. Then one day they set up several tables outdoors. At each table was a prisoner who had been taught to tattoo numbers. She was called a *Schreiber*, a scribe. Truthfully, it felt like being pricked with a pin. The *Schreiber* I had was neat and gentle in her 'work.' Others were rude."

Those selected for work built roads and dug ditches. They sewed uniforms. They worked in factories set up near the camps, making ammunition and parts for airplanes. Many of the factories were run by some of Germany's largest industrial companies. The prisoners worked from morning until night and were hardly fed. Most died within a few months. The dead workers were replaced by others.

Joseph Mandelbaum was chosen for work. It was backbreaking work from early morning until night. And he remembers the food: "To be fifteen, sixteen, years old and to be hungry day and night is something people don't understand. Once a day I ate that piece of bread and soup. I ate it so fast. I was afraid someone would take it from me. I watched them put the soup into my bowl. I hoped it was thick, with a potato maybe, not just water."

Joseph Mandelbaum, 1940.

Hirsh Altusky worked in Skarzysko, Poland, at a hydraulic press. "We had to press highly explosive material into small mines used for land or sea, I don't know which. The chemical used was green and poisonous. After a short while we were covered with it, and you couldn't wash it off. Even our closest friends avoided us like lepers. We worked from six in the morning until six at night. People died standing at the machines. There were explosions. At this work you could not survive more than four, maybe six weeks."

Carol Frenkel Lipson was sent to a labor camp in the

Sudetenland, where she worked at a metal lathe making parts used in German airplanes. She remembers the lack of privacy and decent food at the labor camp, and she remembers the night she and a few other women in her room spoke of their hopes and dreams: "One woman said, 'If I survive, I would want a whole loaf of bread all to myself.' Another said, 'I dream of having a loaf of bread and my own knife to cut it. And I wouldn't eat the crumbs.' Another dreamed of having a loaf of bread, a knife, and her own room. 'Girls, girls, you are so naive,' I told them. 'I dream of having six rooms and plenty of food, not just one loaf of bread.' When they heard that, they were angry with me. How dare I even dream of such a luxury! In those days one didn't even dare to dream of freedom."

Esther Klein remembers how desperate people were for something to eat: "Just before liberation you could feel it in the air, that the Americans were coming. The Nazis didn't give us anything to eat then. No water. No food. Nothing. We just walked around. No one cared who lived or who died."

Leo Fischelberg remembers: "In Bergen-Belsen I saw the Nazis do this more than once. It was a game for them. They hauled two hundred and fifty prisoners into a small barracks, one that should have maybe eighty or ninety people in it. They lit the stove in there real hot. They locked all the doors and windows and stood guard outside for two days. Then they put one kettle of food outside the door, opened it, and watched the starved prisoners trample each other to death as they tried to get out of that hot box and at the food."

The Jews not selected for work were told they needed to be cleaned of lice. They were led to a waiting area made to look like the hall of a bathhouse. Attendants, often dressed in white, distributed towels and pieces of soap. The prisoners were told to undress and to fold their clothes neatly. And they were told to remember where they left their clothes so that after their showers they could reclaim them.

The Jews were crowded into the "bathhouses." There were shower heads and fake drains in the bathhouses, but no water. The "attendants" often shot bullets into the room to force the prisoners to crowd closer together. The doors were locked. SS guards wearing gas masks dropped poison pellets through an opening in the ceiling. Poison fumes filled the room. At times Nazi guards watched through peepholes as innocent men, women, and children gasped and struggled for air in their last moments of life. When the screaming stopped, the Nazis knew the Jews were dead. The gassings took from three to fifteen minutes.

The doors were opened. The bodies were dragged out with metal hooks. Wedding rings were pulled off. Mouths were pried open in search of gold-filled teeth. The gold was sent to the *Reichsbank*, the German national bank. The dead women's hair was used to fill pillows and mattresses. Then the bodies were taken to crematoriums, ovens, where they were burned.

Esther Klein remembers: "In Dachau day and night the crematoriums were burning, day and night they were pushing people in there."

Soon after Cecilia Bernstein came to Auschwitz, she was separated from her mother. She remembers: "Someone said to me, 'You know where your mother is? There.' And she pointed to smoke coming from the chimney."

Lee Potasinski remembers when he first met his block leader in Auschwitz: "He told us, 'None of you will come out alive. The only way out of here is through the chimney.'

A crematorium in the
Bergen-Belsen death camp.

That was a favorite saying in Auschwitz."

Some of the ashes from these ovens were used to fertilize
German gardens. The skin of some dead Jews was used to
make lamp shades. The fat was used to make soap. Hair
was used to make a coarse cloth used in industry. Throughout Germany people wore clothing taken from Jews. German children played with toys taken from Jewish children
who were killed in the death camps.

German industry drew diagrams of the ovens they would
build. They competed to supply the poison, the Zyklon B
gas, used to kill the Jews. German pawnshops bought the

gold from the *Reichsbank*, the gold taken from the teeth of dead Jews.

Horrible medical experiments were performed on some prisoners. Jews were put into pressure chambers until they stopped breathing. They were placed naked in ice water until they froze to death. They were kept in a vacuum until their lungs burst. At Auschwitz the Nazi doctor Josef Mengele was especially brutal. Some three thousand twins suffered through his painful and often deadly experiments. Only 157 survived. Irene Hizme and her twin brother, Rene Slotkin, were among the survivors. Irene Hizme remem-

Eyeglasses taken from prisoners killed in Auschwitz.

bers: "I was a young child then, just five, and he was a doctor. I trusted him. The first time, he took blood from my neck. It was very scary and very painful. But I didn't dare make a sound. If I did, I knew it would be worse. He gave me shots in my back and in my arm, and X rays. Each time I left his laboratory, I was sick, very sick."

Irene Hizme and her twin brother, Rene Slotkin, with their mother, 1942.

Leo Fischelberg was in Auschwitz for seven weeks. Then he was taken to Bergen-Belsen. He remembers those seven weeks in Auschwitz: "I saw kids after the experiments, the twins. I saw boys after castration. I saw girls after experiments. They walked around like they were drunk. I smelled the stench of people dying."

Esther Himmelfarb Peterseil remembers: "We had to stay a certain time under quarantine. After that, at least twice a week, we had selections. That's when I first recognized Josef Mengele, when I first knew who he was. He was tall, slim, and always carried a riding crop. We had to stand straight, with our arms held so our numbers were

Brushes of those
who died at Auschwitz.

showing. He walked behind us and selected people for the
gas. He would point, and someone wrote the numbers
down. A day later they would call the numbers. There was
screaming, crying, praying. We could even hear them when
they were taken to the gas chambers. The noise was so
loud, it was impossible not to hear it."

By late 1942 reports of the death camps reached England,
the United States, and elsewhere. But the media—newspapers, magazines, radio, and newsreels—did little to
spread the news of the killings. Early in 1944 two Jews
escaped Auschwitz and reported in detail about the gas
chambers and the ovens. Allied government officials
seemed almost indifferent to the suffering. In 1944 Allied
bombers were active just a few miles from Auschwitz.
There were many appeals made to Allied leaders to bomb
the railroad tracks leading to the death camp and stop the
deportations, even to bomb the camp itself. But Allied military leaders refused. They claimed they could not spare
the few bombs and the few hours of flying time it would
take to save Jewish lives.

Even as the Jews were brought to the camps, even as they saw the death and dying around them, it was hard for them to believe what was happening. And if the Jews knew their fate, they were almost helpless against Nazi strength. The Nazis had guns, grenades, tanks. Jews who fought back were tortured. But some did fight back. In the Warsaw ghetto a fight began on April 19, 1943, the eve of Passover. Several thousand Jewish men and women, with very few guns and very little food, fought the Nazis.

German soldiers march through the streets of the Warsaw ghetto during the uprising, 1943.

Hirsh Altusky remembers the uprising: "The week before, they allowed us to bake matzo in the ghetto. Then one morning we knew that suddenly something was wrong because the ghetto was surrounded with German and Polish troops. Right away everyone went into the bunkers. Our bunker was in the basement. The entrance to the basement had metal doors and a bar across it. We could lock the door from the inside. Outside was a fake padlock, so if you looked at this, you thought it was closed. There were four rooms down there. The last room had no windows and before the door to the room were shelves, which we put there for camouflage. The shelves had toxic merchandise on them. One day they found the bunker. They knew we were down there. We heard them, voices all around yelling at us to get out. But we stayed quiet. There was even a child with us who had whooping cough, but she never coughed. Then they turned over a kettle with some chemicals in it and smoke came out, so they gave up the search.

"That bunker got burned out during the uprising, so we went to a second bunker, but we went at night. Night was

Jews discovered in the bunkers getting arrested during the Warsaw ghetto uprising.

the only time we could move around, because the Nazis stayed away at night. They were afraid. But we were denounced; someone told the Nazis where to find us. They threw hand grenades in until we yelled that we were coming out."

After forty-two days the Warsaw ghetto uprising ended. The remaining Jews were either killed or deported to the camps.

In August 1943, Jews in the Bialystok ghetto rebelled against the Nazis. Most of those Jews were killed in the fighting. And in September 1943, Nazis with machine guns surrounded the Vilna ghetto. But the Jews fought back. After a week the battle ended. The captured Jews were killed. Many of the Jews who escaped Nazi roundups joined the underground forces that were fighting the Nazis.

Jews fought back in other ghettos too, in Nieswiez, Mir, Lakhua, Tuczyn, Kremenets, Lutsk, Minsk, Stryj, Lublin, Bedzin, and elsewhere. And in a few instances they even fought back in the death camps. There was a small revolt at Treblinka in August 1943. At Sobibor, in October 1943, six hundred prisoners rebelled, killed several Nazi officers, cut telephone wires, and escaped. But only 60 survived the Nazis' chasing after them and the mine fields outside the camp. There was also a revolt at Auschwitz.

Carol Frenkel Lipson was in Auschwitz on October 7, 1944, the day of the revolt. Jewish *Sonderkommando*—prisoners forced to take bodies from the gas chambers—blew up one of the crematoriums, cut the fences, and escaped. "We stood for hours and hours during the siege while they looked for those who had revolted. We saw flames. The crematorium was burning.

"The four girls who were said to have supplied the *Sonderkommando* with explosives smuggled in from the munitions factory they had worked at were later caught and hanged publicly for all to see."

There were acts of heroism during the Holocaust. People in France and Italy helped Jews hide from the Nazis. Catholic priests and nuns in Belgium saved some children. In support of the Jews in Antwerp, Belgium, many Christians wore yellow armbands with Jewish stars sewn on, the same armbands Jews were forced to wear. The Dutch held a general strike to protest Nazi policy. The people of Denmark and Norway helped thousands of Jews escape to Sweden. There were also individual heroes and heroines. Paul Grueninger helped many Jews cross the Austrian border into Switzerland. Father Marie-Benoit saved thousands of French Jews. Sempo Sugihara helped more than two thousand Jews escape the Nazis by issuing Japanese visas to them. Raoul Wallenberg, a Swedish diplomat, saved thousands of Jews in Hungary by issuing them Swedish passports.

Raoul Wallenberg, 1935.

Ivan Gluck remembers the heroism of Raul Wallenberg: "We escaped a roundup of Jews in Nyiregyhaza, Hungary, and went to find Raoul Wallenberg. He was our family's last hope. He gave us false papers and kept us in the Swedish consulate. He saved us. He was an angel of God."

People were heroes in other ways too. Some were killed because they refused to follow Nazi orders. There were pious Jews who continued to observe Jewish law and celebrate Jewish holidays in the ghettos and, in some rare instances, even in the camps. There were people such as Emanuel Ringelblum, who kept diaries so that the world would one day know the horrors of the Holocaust. And there were compassionate heroes like Dr. Janusz Korczak, who eased the pain of the victims.

Dr. Korczak was a physician, an educator, and an author

Father Marie-Benoit

Janusz Korczak.

Erwin Baum, several
weeks after liberation.

of books for children. Beginning in 1911, he was the head of a Jewish home for orphans in Warsaw. In 1942 Korczak and about two hundred of his children were deported to the Treblinka death camp. The Nazis offered to free Korczak, but he refused to leave his children.

Erwin Baum was one of the children in the orphanage. He remembers Korczak: "He was a king, a hero, a superman, a gentle grandpa, everything good a child could imagine. He had such soft hands, with fingers like pillows. When one of us would have a loose tooth, he would take it out so gently. He gave us a coin for the tooth. And from all those teeth he built a tiny castle. When bombs were falling in the ghetto, there was almost no food. On the blackboard it said everyone would get two slices of bread, but he never ate his. Every day he gave away his slices to another child. I was a small boy. I didn't realize he was hungry too, and I took the slices he gave me, which I regret to this day. I would gladly give thirty years of my life to have him here."

Erwin Baum had sneaked outside the ghetto to get food for the orphanage the day the Nazis took Dr. Korczak and the children. "When I saw them take him and the others, I wanted to go to him, but the Germans chased me away. I didn't look Jewish and I spoke Polish well, so the Germans didn't know I was one of the boys."

Erwin Baum was caught later and sent to Auschwitz. He survived the Holocaust. But most European Jews were not so lucky. Every day—and during the summer of 1944, during the night, too—thousands of Jews were murdered.

The Nazis were winning their war against the Jews. But they were losing their war against the allied forces of the United States, Britain, the Soviet Union, and others.

8

"What we saw was horrifying"

June 6, 1944, was D day, the day of the great Allied invasion of Europe. Thousands of American, British, and Canadian soldiers landed on the Normandy beaches, on the northwestern coast of France. The Germans were surprised by the attack, and after several days of heavy fighting and many deaths, the Allies controlled the beach. By the end of the month, 1.5 million Allied soldiers had landed at Normandy. At the same time, Soviet soldiers fought the Germans in the east.

In the months that followed, as the forces against Germany advanced, the Allies liberated Nazi-held Europe and the concentration camps. When they arrived in some camps, the ovens were still warm. The air was still filled with the smell of burning flesh.

Abel Jack Schwartz was a first sergeant with General Patton's Third Army. He was among the first soldiers to liberate Buchenwald. He remembers: "The barracks were inhabited by pitiful, starved prisoners, too weak to move, just skin and bones, living skeletons, and many already dead. The barracks reeked with the scent of human waste

Abel Jack Schwartz, 1945.

Liberated prisoners, 1945.

and death. Outside were heaps of naked bodies like stacks of logs. . . . I had witnessed many battlefield deaths. I considered myself to be tough, and inured to the sight and smell of death. However, at this sight, I just cried and cried. I laid down my pistols, carbine, and grenades out of respect for the dead, and recited the *kaddish*."

In 1945 Arthur Federman was an American soldier fighting in Europe. He entered Dachau a few days after it was liberated. "You could smell the camp from at least five miles away. Until then we didn't even know it was ahead. What

we saw was horrifying. The Jews were emaciated. You could see their bones. They were all skin and bones. There were bodies piled up in tremendous mounds. Practically all the soldiers became nauseous and threw up."

The dead at Bergen-Belsen as they were found when the camp was liberated.

As Allied forces advanced toward the camps, many prisoners were forced by Nazi guards to march, sometimes for hundreds of miles, to territory firmly within control of the German Army. The Nazis were eager to escape, but not without their emaciated prisoners. Those who fell or sat to rest along the way were shot.

א פריילכן פסח

צארי תשז 1947 ... סראניט הנער ...

Leo Machtingier (upper left-hand corner), 1947. This Passover greeting card shows scenes from a Displaced Persons camp in Bari, Italy.

Leo Fischelberg (front row, at right), with other Jewish boys in a Displaced Persons camp, 1946. They are wearing Hitler Youth uniforms, the only clothing available.

Leo Machtingier was in seven different camps. In January 1945 he was forced to march from one camp to another. "There were ten thousand of us when we started. Only about two thousand of us made it. The others were either shot or froze. One night I slept in the middle of five men. Two on the outside never woke up."

Leo Fischelberg was on a thirteen-day march when he was liberated. "A Russian major came riding on horseback along with a lieutenant and a sergeant. They saw men dying from typhoid, with their tongues hanging out. It was not a pretty sight. The lieutenant threw up. The major cried. We tried to comfort them."

Cecilia Bernstein remembers liberation: "Italian workers gave us food. It was meatballs and spaghetti. We were starved. The girls around me ate so much. But their stomachs couldn't take all the food. Many of them died from eating."

After Leo Fischelberg was liberated, he felt lonely. "I was alive, but so many of my friends were gone. I felt like the walking dead. I felt emptiness, nothing else."

After liberation, Judy Schonfeld Schabes traveled back

to her hometown in Hungary. She remembers the train ride: "Whenever someone new came aboard, or I saw someone standing on a platform, I asked, 'Do you know? Did you see? Did you hear? Were you together with so and so?' I hoped to hear about my father. He was only forty-three. Or my mother. She was only thirty-nine. Maybe they were separated out again, before the gas chambers. But they weren't. Of one hundred people in my extended family, just twelve survived."

After the war Esther Himmelfarb Peterseil returned to her hometown in Poland. "I took a trolley to go back to the Jewish community to look for my brother. Then, while I was riding, I saw someone who looked like him. Remember, I hadn't seen him for five years. I called to him. It *was* my brother. He jumped onto the trolley. I don't have to tell you about the reunion. We were both crying, and so was everyone on the trolley." They returned to their apartment. "The building superintendent lived there and wouldn't let us into our own apartment. My brother gave me money to buy some bread, and at the market I saw someone who used to work for our father. It was a thrill for me to see her, but she said, 'Are you still alive?' She wasn't pleased to see me."

Esther Himmelfarb Peterseil with two other survivors, 1946.

Judy Schonfeld Schabes had a very different experience after liberation. She remembers: "Just before we went to Auschwitz, my father gave to some very fine Christian neighbors our furs, jewelry, silverware, and money and told them, 'Do what you want with this. It's yours.' After the war these people saw me and said, 'Daddy gave this to us, but it's yours.' And they gave it all back to me."

Ivan Gluck returned to Nyiregyhaza, Hungary. Of the thirty boys in his small school, only five survived. He remembers: "I saw ashes, soap made from human fat, hair, and lamp shades made from skin brought back from the camps. These remains, the soap, hair, and lamp shades, were all buried in the Jewish cemetery."

And what was to happen to the Jews who survived, those still alive when the camps were liberated, those who were hiding in Christian homes, in sewers, or in forests? There was still no place for them. Their homes and families were gone. They were called Displaced Persons, and no country wanted them.

Camps for these Displaced Persons were set up in Germany, Austria, and Italy. The camps were guarded and surrounded with barbed wire. Many Jews still wore their prisoner uniforms. Some were given abandoned SS uniforms to wear. In August 1945 the American representative on a refugee committee, Earl G. Harrison, inspected the camps. He reported, "As matters now stand, we appear to be treating the Jews as the Nazis treated them, except that we do not exterminate them." After reading this report, President Truman of the United States ordered that treatment of the Jews in the camps be improved.

During the first months of 1946 there were about seventy-five thousand Jews in the camps. But because of a tragic attack on July 4, 1946, there was soon a large increase in the population of these camps.

Two hundred Jews had returned either from hiding or from concentration camps to rebuild the Jewish community in Kielce, Poland. On July 3, 1946, Polish police took away their weapons. The next day Polish citizens attacked the Jews. They pelted the Jews with stones and shot at them. They clubbed Jews to death. Forty-two were killed. Many others were wounded. When news of this attack became known, thousands of Jewish survivors fled from towns and villages throughout Poland to Displaced Persons camps.

By 1947 there were two hundred and fifty thousand Jews in the camps.

Most of the survivors in the camps wanted to leave quickly, to resettle outside Europe. And people who lived near the camps were eager to have the Jews leave. Leah Goldberg was in a camp in Germany and heard one of the local citizens say, "Where did all these Jews come from? I thought we killed them all."

Jews in a German Displaced Persons camp demonstrating for open emigration to Palestine.

Only a fraction of the many who wanted to enter the United States, Britain, and Palestine were allowed in. It was only in 1948, with the establishment of the state of Israel, that many of these Jews found a home.

9

"Tell them I was there. I'm real. It happened"

The anti-Jewish policies of the Nazis were widely known as early as the 1920s, when Hitler first began attracting a following. And even before the liberation of the death camps, the camps' true nature was certainly known to leaders of various governments and to the media. But much of what was reported about the camps was hidden in the middle pages of newspapers and magazines. Average citizens in countries not overrun by Germany may have had only a vague knowledge of what was happening. But in April 1945, when photographs of the victims filled newspapers and magazines and were shown on newsreels, the world truly understood the horrors of the Holocaust.

In the months and years since liberation, thousands of Nazis have been brought to trial. The first trials were at Nuremberg, Germany. On November 20, 1945, when twenty-two leading Nazis were accused of "crimes against humanity," the Nazis claimed they were blameless, that they were only following orders. Ten and a half months later the trials ended, and nineteen of the twenty-two were found guilty. Seven were imprisoned. Twelve were executed.

The trials at Nuremberg.

In April 1947, Alfred Lipson was a witness at one of the later trials at Nuremberg. He remembers: "I was more anguished sitting there, waiting to testify, than the prisoners. I imagined them sitting there full of regret. But no, they hoped to escape punishment. They seemed almost smug."

On December 9, 1946, at one of the first trials in Nuremberg, Germany, U.S. Brigadier General Telford Taylor made an opening statement that included an explanation of the importance of the trials. "The mere punishment of the defendants," he said, "or even thousands of others equally guilty, can never redress the terrible injuries which the Nazis visited on these unfortunate peoples. For them it is far more important that these incredible events be established by clear and public proof, so that no one can ever doubt that they were fact and not fable."

Hermann Göring on trial at Nuremberg, 1946.

U.S. Brigadier General Telford Taylor.

Al Feuerstein's passport, 1946.

The chief British prosecutor, Sir Hartley Shawcross, said of the Holocaust, "History holds no parallel to these horrors." And Hans Frank, the former general governor of Nazi-occupied Poland and one of the defendants at Nuremberg, declared, "A thousand years will pass and this guilt of Germany will still not be erased."

The guilt may not be ereased, but as time passes, people forget. The survivors, however, did not and cannot forget. Even today their memories haunt them.

Al Feuerstein remembers when he came to the United States, in 1946: "I was afraid. I was afraid to be a Jew. My friends told me, 'Don't worry. We have a constitution. It can never happen again.' I said, 'Germany was a democracy. It had a constitution too.'"

Shulamit Erlebacher remembers: "My parents were sent to the Warsaw ghetto and were later killed. My aunt died in Auschwitz. She was the one who raised me. My two sisters died working in coal mines. My brother died in Dachau with his wife and child. Sometimes I ask, 'Why was I the only one to survive?'"

More than forty years after Irene Hizme and her brother, Rene Slotkin, were separated from their mother, they found her death certificate. It was in a small museum in Israel. Rene Slotkin remembers: "I felt a terrible sadness for her and for me. And that terrible moment of separation came back to me. I heard my mother crying out. It was difficult, very difficult, to walk away from that paper."

Memories of the Holocaust intrude every day on Irene Hizme. "Every time I take a shower, I think of Auschwitz. There's a great deal of sadness in my life because of the Holocaust."

Esther Himmelfarb Peterseil is not free from the past. "I have nightmares. I remind myself of something and it brings tears to my eyes. I'm more touchy. I'm afraid of gentiles. Since Auschwitz, I have never taken a shower, only baths."

And Judy Schonfeld Schabes is not free from the past. "Every time we have a cookout, I say, 'There is that smell.' I'm forever thinking what I would be like today if I hadn't gone through it, if a single parent had survived, or a sibling. I'm very overprotective of my family now."

Ernest Honig's daughter once asked him, "Daddy, did you have a mommy?" All her friends had grandparents. She didn't.

Clara Wachter Feldman is still not free from the past. "I go to a bar mitzvah now and think of all the bar mitzvahs that have never been, the children who will never be. I'm ambivalent about my own survival. The happiest years since 1933 were the years I was raising my children. Then I was making a statement. They didn't defeat us."

Aron Hirt-Manheimer was born in a Displaced Persons camp in Feldafing, Germany. He is the child of survivors. He remembers: "I felt rage. I felt my parents were dishonored, humiliated. I felt I had to fight back, but there was no one to fight. Later I became active in the effort to track down and prosecute escaped Nazi war criminals. I feel privileged to be the child of survivors. I represent the future of many people who perished: my aunts, my uncles, and their children. It is a tremendous responsibility.

"My parents called me their *oytzer*, their treasure. But I was also their helper. I taught them English. I taught them how to drive. I had to contribute to their healing. My sister and I proved that Hitler had not destroyed the Jewish family. We meant continuity."

Florence Bauman Wiener is the daughter of Holocaust survivors. She grew up without grandparents, aunts, un-

Renee and Victor Schonfeld, the parents of Judy Schonfeld Schabes, 1926.

Aron Hirt-Manheimer (second from left), with his family, 1959.

cles, or cousins. "Both my parents came from large families. I don't know how large. They were both married to other people and had children. But only my parents survived. They met and married in Bergen-Belsen in 1945 after liberation. The death camp had become a Displaced Persons camp. That's where my brother Jacob and I were born. When I was eight, someone asked me where I was born, and I said, 'Bergen-Belsen.' To me that was as natural as saying Brooklyn or Staten Island."

Florence Bauman Wiener (at right), with her mother and brother in a Displaced Persons camp in Bergen-Belsen, 1950.

Florence Bauman Wiener's parents were very protective. She remembers: "My mother never wanted to let me out of her sight. When I was sixteen, I was going to the beach with friends. My mother said she would follow me. She said she would sit far away on a bench and watch. No one would even know she was there. My mother often said, 'You should never have to know why I feel the way I do.'"

Auschwitz remains as a museum and a monument. Erwin Baum returned there in June 1988. "I hired a taxi and went to the camp. I went to the bunk where I slept. I went to where they put on my number. I went to the bench where they beat us. When I was thirteen and went there for the first time, there was no way out. This time I walked in because I wanted to, and on the other side of the gate there was a taxi waiting for me whenever I was ready to leave. I felt truly liberated for the first time. I had walked in and out with my own free will. To the people who say there was no Holocaust, tell them I was there. I'm real. It happened."

As a result of mistreatment by the Nazis, Aron Hirt-Manheimer's father contracted tuberculosis. After the war he spent several years in a sanatorium but had trouble breathing for the rest of his life. He died in 1984. Aron Hirt-Manheimer remembers his father: "Even if he wanted, my father couldn't hide the scars. His body was a map of the Holocaust. He was shot with a machine gun while trying to escape the train which was taking him to Auschwitz, and his back was bent from the bullets which left their mark on his back and chest. He had a number, a blue tattoo, on his left arm. Because he had been beaten so often, he had a permanent black-and-blue mark on his knuckles. The pain he endured was unbelievable. But my father did not give up on humanity. He continued to care about others and refused to judge people collectively.

"Twenty years ago I escorted my father on his only trip to Israel. Ironically, our itinerary called for a stopover in Frankfurt. As we filed into the airport terminal, we saw uniformed German sentinels all around us. 'Damn murderers,' I whispered. 'We never should have come here.' My father turned to me and said in Yiddish, '*Aron, nish alle Deutschen zenen gevein schlecht*—Aron, not all Germans were bad.' He tried to pass on to us, to me and my sister Rose, all the best values of Judaism, to be a *mensch* [a

Aron Hirt-Manheimer's parents at their wedding, 1947.

Victims of the Holocaust.

The Svwalki Strelecki family, victims of the Holocaust.

decent, honorable person]. 'You be what you want others to be.' "

People who have read about and studied the history of the Holocaust wonder how a tragedy of such unparalleled dimensions could have occurred. Historians, philosophers, religious thinkers, have asked, "Where was God? Where was man?"

"Where was God?" is a difficult, perhaps impossible, question to answer. Some feel it is not even a proper question to ask. But "Where was man?" Where were the basically good people of this world, the people who consider themselves free of prejudice and hate, the people who would never willfully harm others?

These people were in many places. They were at home in the 1930s, calmly reading newspaper reports of the weather, of baseball games, and of Jews losing their rights as citizens of Germany. They were standing outside Jewish-owned stores in Germany on April 1, 1933, but they did not go in. These people were watching as Jews were forced from their homes and into ghettoes. They were standing by and watching as Jews were rounded up and taken off in locked cattle cars. They were living near enough to the death camps to smell the burning flesh. They were in positions of leadership with the power to help but not caring enough to stop the massacre. There were good, brave people too, who were protesting the discrimination, helping people to escape, and hiding Jews from the Nazis at great personal risk.

No words, no book, can fully describe the humiliation, the pain, the horror, of that time. The lives lost cannot be reclaimed. And still the lesson the Holocaust has to teach us has not been learned. Prejudice, bigotry, and hatred have not disappeared. On the contrary, in the past few years violent acts motivated by prejudice have increased. And often the people guilty of painting swastikas on Jewish buildings, of attacking Jews, blacks, and others, are young people.

People today must learn not to hate, to teach their children not to hate. They must understand that hatred can lead to discrimination and violence. What happened once must not happen again.

Aaron Tibor Katz of Romania, victim of the Holocaust.

Chronology

Important Dates, 1933–1945

1933

January 30   Adolf Hitler is appointed chancellor of Germany.

February 27–28   Fire destroys the *Reichstag*. All one hundred Communist party members of the *Reichstag* are arrested.

March 23   The first concentration camp opens, in Dachau, a German town near Munich.

March 27   In response to a planned boycott of Jewish-owned stores and businesses in Germany, 55,000 people protest at a rally in New York City's Madison Square Garden, and those present threaten to boycott all German goods. Nazis change their plans and limit their boycott to one day.

Adolf Hitler.

The German boycott of Jewish businesses.

April 1	Boycott in Germany of Jewish-owned stores and businesses.
April 7	Jewish government workers are ordered to retire.
April 26	The Gestapo, the German secret police, is established.
May 10	Books written by Jews and opponents of Nazism are burned.
June 27	Mass Jewish rally in London to protest Nazi anti-Semitism.
July 14	Nazi party declared the only legal party in Germany.
October 14	Germany withdraws from the League of Nations.

October 27	Arabs in Palestine riot to protest Jewish immigration there.

1934

April 7	Several thousand attend a pro-Nazi rally in Queens, New York.
May 17	More than 20,000 people attend a pro-Nazi rally at Madison Square Garden in New York.
June 30–July 2	Night of the Long Knives. Leaders of the SA (Brown Shirts), once among Hitler's closest friends and allies, are killed by the SS (Black Shirts) on Hitler's orders.
August 2	Paul von Hindenburg, president of Germany, dies. Hitler becomes president and commander-in-chief of the armed forces.

1935

March 16	Hitler rejects the Treaty of Versailles and begins to draft Germans into military service.
May 31	Jews may no longer serve in the German Army.
June	Anti-Jewish riots in Poland.
September 15	The Nuremberg Laws are passed. Among them are laws denying Jews citizenship in Germany. The Nazi symbol, a black swastika within a round white

Early Nazi flags.

field on red cloth, becomes the official German flag.

November 15   German law defines a Jew as anyone who considers himself a Jew and has two Jewish grandparents, or anyone with three or more Jewish grandparents whether he considers himself a Jew or not.

1936

February 4   Swiss Nazi leader Wilhelm Gustloff is assassinated as a reprisal for Nazi anti-Semitism.

March 3   Jewish doctors no longer allowed to work in German government hospitals.

March 7   German troops march into the Rhineland in violation of the Treaty of Versailles.

April 21   Arabs riot in Tel Aviv–Jaffa to protest Jewish immigration to Palestine.

June 30   Polish Jews strike to protest anti-Semitism.

October 25   Hitler and Mussolini sign treaty, forming Rome-Berlin Axis.

1937

March 15   Large anti-Nazi rally in New York City.

July 16   Buchenwald concentration camp opens.

September 5   Hitler views parade of 600,000 German soldiers in Nuremberg.

November 25	Germany and Japan sign military agreement.

1938

January 21	Jews in Romania lose their rights as citizens.
March 13	The *Anschluss*. The German Army marches into Austria. German anti-Semitic decrees now apply to the Jews in Austria.
April 26	All Jewish property must be registered with the Nazis.
May 29	Anti-Jewish laws passed in Hungary.
July 5	Evian Conference on German refugees opens.
August 17	German Jewish women must add "Sara" to their names. Men must add "Israel."
September 29–30	At the Munich Conference the leaders of Britain and France agree that Germany may annex the Sudetenland.
October 5	All German Jews must have their passports marked with a large red *J*.
October 28	Polish Jews living in Germany are expelled.
November 7	In Paris, Herschel Grynszpan shoots Ernst vom Rath, a German embassy employee.
November 9	*Kristallnacht*, the Night of Broken

A Jewish woman's identification papers, 1938. Note the word "Sara" added to the name, and the large *J* for "*Juden*."

A synagogue burns on *Kristallnacht*.

Glass. Many thousands of Jewish-owned stores and businesses are broken into and robbed. Synagogues are burned. Jews are arrested and degraded. Some are killed.

November 15 — Jewish children may no longer attend German schools.

1939

January 30 — In a speech before the German parliament, Hitler declares that if there is war, the Jews of Europe will be destroyed.

February 9 — Anti-Jewish laws are passed in Italy.

March 15 — Germans occupy Bohemia and Moravia (regions of Czechoslovakia).

March 25 — In New York, 20,000 people march in a huge public "Stop Hitler" protest while an estimated 500,000 line the streets and watch.

August 23 — Germany and the Soviet Union sign the Molotov-Ribbentrop Pact, agreeing not to attack each other.

September 1 — The German Army invades Poland. World War II begins.

September 3 — France and Britain declare war on Germany.

September 27 — German orders are issued to establish ghettos in Poland.

October 24	Jews in Wloclawek, Poland, are required to wear a large yellow triangle.
October 30	The British government publishes a report of Nazi brutality in concentration camps.
November 23	Polish Jews are ordered to wear in public at all times armbands with yellow Stars of David.
November 28	A ghetto is set up in Piotrkow, the first in Poland.

1940

February 8	Orders are issued to set up a ghetto in Lodz, Poland.
April 9	The German Army invades Denmark and Norway.
April 27	Orders are issued to set up a concentration camp at Auschwitz, Poland.
May 1	The Lodz ghetto is established.
May 10	The German Army invades Holland, Belgium, and France.

A woman selling Star of David armbands. The armbands had to be paid for by Jews.

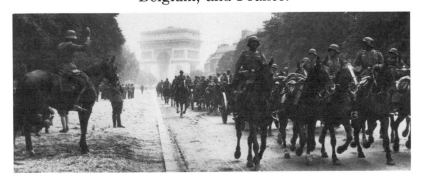

The German Army marches into France.

June 4	French and British troops are evacuated from Dunkirk.
June 22	France surrenders to Germany.
September 27	Japan signs a treaty with Germany and Italy, forming the Rome-Berlin-Tokyo Axis.
November 15	Walls surrounding the Warsaw ghetto are completed and closed.

1941

June 22	The German Army invades the Soviet Union. *Einsatzgruppen* (Nazi murder squads) begin mass killings of Soviet Jews.
June 28	Red Friday. Nazis burn the Jewish section in Bialystok, Poland. More than 1,000 Jews, forced into the synagogue, are killed.
July 31	Reinhard Heydrich is appointed to carry out German anti-Semitic strategy.
September 1	Jews in Germany are required to wear a yellow star on their clothing.
September 28	Murder of Jews at Babi Yar (near Kiev, in the Ukraine) begins. More than 30,000 will be killed in two days.
October 15	Orders are issued that any Jew in Poland found outside a ghetto will be shot.
December 7	The Japanese attack Pearl Harbor, Ha-

The Japanese attack Pearl Harbor.

waii. The United States declares war on Japan.

December 8	Mass killings begin at Chelmno death camp.
December 11	Germany and Italy declare war on the United States.

1942

January 20	At the Wannsee Conference plans are developed by the Nazis for the total destruction of the Jews in Europe, the "Final Solution."
February 24	The *S.S. Struma*, a small boat with 769 Romanian Jewish refugees on board, sinks in the Black Sea.
March 1	Gas chambers begin operations at Sobibor. Trains begin to arrive at Auschwitz.

March 17	Killings begin in the Belzec, Poland, death camp.
June 1	Treblinka death camp opens.
June 30	Jewish schools in Germany are closed.
July 22	Deportations from Warsaw ghetto to Treblinka begin.
July 28	The Jewish Fighting Organization (ZOB) is established in the Warsaw ghetto.
December 22	Jewish resistance fighters in Krakow, Poland, attack German troops.

1943

January 18	Jewish resistance begins in the Warsaw ghetto.
February 5	Jewish resistance begins in the Bialystok ghetto.

German soldiers watching as the Warsaw ghetto burns.

114

April 19	The Warsaw ghetto revolt begins.
	At the Bermuda Conference, U.S. and British representatives discuss resettlement of refugees from Nazi persecution. No action is taken.
June 11	Heinrich Himmler orders all Jews in Polish ghettos to be sent to camps.
June 21	Himmler orders all Jews in Russian ghettos to be sent to camps.
August 2	Rebellion of inmates in Treblinka.
August 16	Revolt begins in the Bialystok, Poland, ghetto.
October 2	The Danish underground helps 7,000 Jews escape to Sweden.
October 14	Prisoners revolt at the Sobibor death camp.

1944

May–June	An estimated 400,000 Hungarian Jews killed at Auschwitz.
June 6	D day, the Allied invasion of Nazi-held Europe.
July 20	German Army officers attempt to assassinate Hitler, but fail.
July 24	Soviet forces discover abandoned Maidanek death camp.
October 7	Revolt in Auschwitz.

American soldiers landing
at Normandy.

A monument to an
American soldier killed at
Normandy.

November 8	Death march of Jews from Budapest to Austria begins.

1945

January 17	Death march from Auschwitz begins. Raoul Wallenberg is arrested by Soviet police in Budapest. His fate remains unknown.
April 15	Bergen-Belsen is liberated by the British.
April 25	Invading American forces from the west and Soviet forces from the east meet in Torgau, Germany.
April 29	Dachau is liberated by American troops.
April 30	Hitler commits suicide.
May 8	Germany surrenders to Allies.
November 22	Nuremberg Trials of Nazis begin.

Glossary

Mordecai Anielewicz.

Allies: The nations, including the United States, Britain, France, and the Soviet Union, that joined in the fight in World War II against Germany and the other Axis nations.

Anielewicz, Mordecai (1919–43): Jewish leader of the Warsaw ghetto uprising.

Anschluss: The 1938 German invasion and annexation of Austria.

anti-Semitism: Prejudice against Jews.

Appeasement: The policy adopted by European leaders in the late 1930s of giving in to Hitler's demands in order to avoid war.

Aryan: An ancient people of Central Asia. Used by the Nazis to mean a superior, white gentile.

Auschwitz-Birkenau: Nazi labor and death camp located in Poland.

Axis: The nations, including Italy and Japan, that fought in World War II alongside Germany against the Allies.

Baeck, Leo (1873–1956): Rabbi and a leader of German Jewry during the Holocaust period.

Leo Baeck.

117

bar mitzvah: A Jewish boy on his thirteenth birthday is called a bar mitzvah, which means he has reached his religious maturity. There is often a party to celebrate this event. (A Jewish girl reaching her religious maturity is called a bat mitzvah.)

Belzec: Nazi death camp located in eastern Poland.

bench gomel: Jewish prayer of thanks expressed by someone who has safely passed through great danger.

Bergen-Belsen: Nazi concentration camp located in Germany.

Bermuda Conference: The meeting between U.S. and British government representatives in 1943 at which the problem of refugees of Nazi persecution was discussed.

Blitzkrieg: German for "lightning war."

Bormann, Martin (1900– ?):   A close advisor to Adolf Hitler. Sentenced to death at the Nuremberg Trials, but his whereabouts after the war and fate are unknown.

Braun, Eva (1912–45):   Adolf Hitler's mistress. They married on April 12, 1945, shortly before they committed suicide.

Buchenwald: Nazi concentration camp located near Weimar, Germany.

cantor: Leader of synagogue prayer.

Chamberlain, Neville (1869–1940):   Prime Minister of Britain, 1937–40, most remembered for his policy of appeasing Hitler and Mussolini to avoid war. Resigned May 10, 1940.

Chelmno: The first Nazi death camp in Poland.

Churchill, Sir Winston (1874–1965):   Prime Minister of Britain during most of World War II (May 1940–July 1945) and again after the war (1951–55). Led his country in the fight against Germany.

concentration camp: A prison in which "enemies of the German nation" were concentrated. Before the end of World War II, more than one hundred such camps had been set up.

crematorium: Oven in which death-camp victims' bodies were burned.

Dachau: The first Nazi concentration camp, near Munich, Germany.

Daladier, Edouard (1884–1970): Premier of France (1933–34, and 1938–40). Signed the Munich Agreement in 1938 in an effort to appease Hitler and avoid war. Was arrested by the Nazis after the defeat of France and held prisoner until 1945.

Dannecher, Theodor (1913–45): SS captain responsible for deporting Jews from France, Bulgaria, and Italy to Nazi death camps.

death camps: Camps built to kill Jews and other "enemies of the German nation." There were six death camps: Auschwitz, Belzec, Chelmno, Maidanek, Sobibor, and Treblinka.

death marches: Near the end of the war, as the Soviet Army moved in from the east, Nazi SS forced prisoners in concentration and death camps located in Poland to march to camps located in Germany.

deportation: The Jews' forced relocation from their homes to other places, usually ghettos or Nazi camps.

Dora-Nordhausen: Nazi concentration camp located in Germany.

Eichmann, Adolf (1906–62): SS officer who directed roundup of Jews and their transport to concentration and death camps.

Glossary

Einsatzgruppen: Killing squads. Mobile killing units of the SS that followed the German Army into Poland and the Soviet Union.

Final Solution: The Nazi term for their plan to murder every Jew in Europe.

Flossenbürg: Nazi concentration camp located in Germany.

Prisoners at Flossenbürg.

Frank, Hans (1900–46): Nazi governor general of Poland, 1939–45. Tried and executed as a war criminal in Nuremberg.

Führer: German for "leader." Used in reference to Adolf Hitler.

gas chambers: Sealed rooms in the death camps. Jewish prisoners were crowded into these rooms and poison gas was released, killing the prisoners.

genocide: The systematic killing of a nation or race of people.

gentile: Non-Jew.

German-American Bund: Anti-Semitic organization established in the United States in 1933 as Friends of the New Germany and renamed in 1936. Held rallies, distributed anti-Semitic literature and encouraged the boycott of Jews and Jewish-owned businesses. Membership in the Bund declined in 1939, when World War II began.

Gestapo: The Nazi secret police.

ghetto: The part of a city in which Jews were forced to live.

Goebbels, Joseph (1897–1945): Chief of Nazi propaganda. Committed suicide, 1945.

Göring, Hermann (1893–1946): Commander of the German Air Force and Deputy Chancellor of Nazi Germany. Sentenced to death at Nuremberg Trials; committed suicide, 1946.

Gross-Rosen: Nazi concentration camp located in Poland.

Grüber, Heinrich (1891–1975): German Protestant leader who risked his life to save Jews from Nazi persecution.

Gurs: Nazi concentration camp located in France.

Heine, Heinrich (1797–1856): German-Jewish author and poet.

Hess, Rudolf (1894–1987): An aide to Hitler. Flew on his own to Scotland in 1941 seeking peace. Remained there until the end of the war and was then sentenced to life in prison.

Heydrich, Reinhard (1904–42): Deputy head of SS, he directed the *Einsatzgruppen* and planned the "Final Solution." Assassinated in Czechoslovakia by the Czech resistance.

Himmler, Heinrich (1900–45): Head of the SS. Committed suicide, 1945.

Paul von Hindenburg.

Hindenburg, Paul von (1847–1934): German military hero during World War I and president of Germany, 1925–34.

Hitler, Adolf (1889–1945): Nazi party leader, 1919–45. German chancellor, 1933–45. Committed suicide in a Berlin bunker.

Hitler Youth: Nazi youth organization. From 1936 the only legal youth organization in Nazi Germany.

Holocaust: "Destruction by fire." Sometime after the end of Nazi rule in Germany, the word came to be used to refer to the Nazi killing of six million Jews, in the years 1933–45.

Höss, Rudolf (1900–47): Chief administrator of Auschwitz, 1940–43. Sentenced to death at Nuremberg Trials.

Juden: German word for "Jews."

Judenrat: "Jewish council." Jews appointed by the Germans to govern the ghettos.

judenrein: German for "free of Jews."

kaddish: A prayer praising God. Recited by Jewish mourners.

kapos: Prisoners within concentration camps who were selected by the Nazis to oversee other prisoners.

Keitel, Wilhelm (1882–1946): German Army officer, chief of staff to Hitler throughout World War II. Signed the surrender of Germany, May 8, 1945. Sentenced to death at Nuremberg Trials.

Korczak, Janusz (1878–1942): Educator, author, and director of a Jewish orphanage in Warsaw. Despite an offer of personal freedom, refused to abandon his orphans and went with them to his death in Treblinka.

Kristallnacht: "Night of Broken Glass." November 9–11, 1938, when there were wholesale arrests of Jews and destruction of Jewish property in Germany and Austria.

labor camp: A Nazi concentration camp in which the prisoners were used as slave laborers.

Leopold III (1901–83): King of Belgium, 1934–51. Held prisoner of war by Germany, 1940–45.

Luftwaffe: German Air Force.

Luftwaffe bombers.

Maidanek: Nazi labor and death camp located in Poland.

matzo: Flat, crackerlike bread not given time to rise. Eaten on Passover in remembrance of what the Jews ate as they fled slavery in Egypt.

Mauthausen: Nazi concentration camp located in Austria.

Mengele, Josef (1911–77): The medical doctor and SS captain who at Auschwitz made "selections" and conducted sadistic medical experiments on prisoners. Escaped to Paraguay after the war, where he died of natural causes.

Mein Kampf: "My Struggle." Title of a book by Adolf Hitler, written in 1924, outlining his plans for Germany.

Müller, Heinrich (1896– ?): Gestapo chief, 1939–45. Directly responsible for carrying out the "Final Solution." Whereabouts after the war and fate unknown.

Mussolini, Benito (1883–1945): Absolute ruler of Italy, 1922–43, and an ally of Adolf Hitler. Killed by his enemies in 1945.

Natzweiler: Nazi concentration camp located in France.

Neuengamme: Nazi concentration camp located in Germany.

Orthodox Jews: Traditional Jews who follow the many precepts of the Torah, including the eating of only Kosher foods and observing the laws of the Sabbath.

Passover: The Jewish holiday celebrating the Jews' exodus from Egypt, where they had been slaves, in ancient times. Celebrated beginning on the fourteenth of the Hebrew month of Nissan (March-April).

Purim: Jewish   holiday   celebrating   the   rescue   from

Purim party, Lithuania, 1935.

Haman, prime minister of ancient Persia, who had intended to kill every Jew in the empire. Celebrated on the fourteenth of the Jewish month of Adar (February-March).

Putsch: German word meaning armed revolt.

Rascher, Sigmund (1909–45): Nazi doctor who performed sadistic medical experiments on prisoners at Dachau. Reported shot at Dachau.

Ravensbrück: Nazi concentration camp for women located in Germany.

Reichstag: The German parliament, and the building in which it met.

Ribbentrop, Joachim von (1893–1946): German foreign minister. Negotiated an agreement between the Soviet Union and Germany in 1939 that neither country would attack the other.

Righteous of the Nations: Righteous gentiles. The term used for gentiles who risked their lives to save Jews from Nazi persecution. At Yad Vashem in Jerusalem there is an avenue lined with trees: Each tree was planted to commemorate a righteous gentile. Among the hundreds honored are Raoul Wallenberg, Paul Grueninger, Oskar Schindler, Sempo Sugihara, Marion Pritchard, and Angelo Roncalli (who later became Pope John XXIII).

Röhm, Ernst (1887–1934): Head of the SA. Taken prisoner by the SS on June 30, 1934 (Night of the Long Knives), and murdered by them two days later.

Roosevelt, Franklin Delano (1882–1945): U.S. President from March 1933 until his death in April 1945, almost the entire period of Nazi rule in Germany.

Rosh Hashanah: The Jewish New Year, celebrated on the first day of the Hebrew month of Tishri (September-October).

Avenue of the Righteous, Yad Vashem, Jerusalem.

SA: *Sturmabteilung,* storm troopers, or Brown Shirts. Organized to protect Nazi rallies and to terrorize those not sympathetic to the Nazis.

Sabbath: The weekly day of rest beginning before sunset on Friday and ending after sunset on Saturday. Traditional Jews do no work on the Sabbath.

Sachsenhausen: Nazi concentration camp located in Germany.

scapegoat: An innocent person or people blamed for other people's troubles.

Schirach, Baldur von (1907–74): Head of Hitler Youth. Sentenced to twenty years in prison.

SD: *Sicherheitsdienst,* or security police. Established in 1931 as a section of the SS. Administered the death camps and were the *Einsatzgruppen,* or killing squads.

selection: The process of deciding which prisoners in Nazi camps would be sent to their deaths immediately and which would be spared.

Shawcross, Sir Hartley (1902–   ): British chief prosecutor at Nuremberg Trials.

Sobibor: Nazi death camp located in Poland.

Sonderkommando: Prisoners in the death camps assigned to take the bodies from the gas chambers to the crematoriums.

SS: *Schutzstaffel,* protection squad, or Black Shirts. Established in 1925 as Nazi protection squads. Included the Gestapo; squads that ran the Nazi concentration and death camps; and squads that fought with the German Army.

Stalin, Joseph (1879–1953): Dictator of the Soviet Union 1929–53.

Stauffenberg, Claus (1907–44): Leader of the German oppositon to Hitler who, in 1944, placed a time bomb beneath Hitler's table. Hitler survived the assassination attempt, and Stauffenberg was executed.

Streicher, Julius (1885–1946): Publisher of *Der Stürmer* ("The Great Storm"), an anti-Semitic newspaper published in Germany, 1923–45. Tried and executed in Nuremberg.

Stroop, Jürgen (1895–1951): SS general responsible for the destruction of the Warsaw ghetto.

Stutthof: Nazi concentration camp located in Poland.

Sudetenland: The western section of Czechoslovakia, which borders on Germany.

swastika: An old religious ornament, adopted by the Nazis as their party symbol.

tallis: Rectangular cloth with specially prepared fringes *(tzitzit).* Worn by Jews during prayer.

Taylor, Telford (1908–   ): American lawyer and army officer during World War II and American chief prosecutor at the Nuremberg Trials.

Terezin: Also known as Theresienstadt. Nazi concentration camp located in Czechoslovakia. Set up to show the outside world, including Red Cross investigators, how well the Jews were being treated. Most Jews held here were later killed in Auschwitz.

Third Reich: Hitler's name for Germany during his years as dictator, 1933–45.

Treaty of Versailles: Peace treaty that ended World War I.

Treblinka: Nazi death camp located in Poland.

Wallenberg, Raoul (1912– ?): Businessman who worked at the Swedish embassy in Budapest, Hungary, and saved the lives of thousands of Jews. Captured by So-

Train station at Treblinka.

viet troops in 1945. His whereabouts and fate are unknown.

War Refugee Board: U.S. agency established in 1944 to rescue victims of Nazi persecution.

Wehrmacht: The German Army.

Weimar Republic: The German democratic government from 1919–34.

Weissmandel, Michael (1903–57): Hungarian rabbi who escaped from a train bound for Auschwitz. Pleaded with the Allies in vain that the tracks leading to the death camps be bombed.

Wiesel, Elie (1928–   ): Holocaust survivor who has written many works relating to the Holocaust. Awarded the Nobel Peace Prize in 1986.

Wiesenthal, Simon (1908–   ): Holocaust survivor who has helped capture and prosecute more than one thousand Nazi war criminals.

Yad Vashem: Memorial in Jerusalem to Holocaust victims, and center for Holocaust study.

Glossary

yarmulke: Small cap worn on the head of traditional Jews, especially while praying and eating, as a sign of respect for God.

Yiddish: Also know as Jewish. The language spoken by the majority of East European Jews before World War II.

Yom Kippur: The Jewish Day of Atonement, a fast day spent mostly in prayer. Falls on the tenth of the Jewish month of Tishri (September-October).

Zionist: Supporter of the establishment of a Jewish homeland in the land area that is now Israel.

ZOB: The Warsaw ghetto Jewish fighting organization.

Zyklon B: The gas used to kill Jews in the death camps.

Suggested Reading

There are many excellent books on the Holocaust for young readers. Your librarian will be able to help you to make selections, as well as inform you of newly published books. The following list is not comprehensive but is a good first look at some of the books currently available.

NONFICTION

Abells, Chana Byers. *The Children We Remember*. New York: Greenwillow, 1987.

Altshuler, David. *Hitler's War Against the Jews*. New York: Behrman House, 1978. (A young readers' edition of *The War Against the Jews*, by Lucy S. Dawidowicz.)

Auerbacher, Inge. *I Am a Star: Child of the Holocaust*. New York: Prentice-Hall, 1985.

Bernbaum, Israel. *My Brother's Keeper: The Holocaust Through the Eyes of an Artist*. New York: G.P. Putnam, 1985.

Chaikin, Miriam. *A Nightmare in History: The Holocaust 1933–1945*. New York: Clarion, 1987.

Frank, Anne. *The Diary of a Young Girl*. New York: Doubleday, 1952.

Greene, Carol. *Elie Wiesel: Messenger from the Holocaust*. Chicago: Children's Press, 1987.

Hautzig, Esther. *The Endless Steppe*. New York: Thomas Y. Crowell, 1968.

Suggested Reading

Herman, Erwin, and Herman, Agnes. *The Yanov Torah*. Rockville, Maryland: Kar-Ben Copies, 1985.

Isaacman, Clara. *Clara's Story*. Philadelphia: Jewish Publication Society, 1984.

Joffo, Joseph. *A Bag of Marbles*. Boston: Houghton Mifflin, 1974.

Kluger, Ruth, and Mann, Peggy. *The Secret Ship*. New York: Doubleday, 1978.

Meltzer, Milton. *Never to Forget: The Jews of the Holocaust*. New York: Harper & Row, 1976.

Reiss, Johanna. *The Upstairs Room*. New York: Thomas Y. Crowell, 1972.

Rogasky, Barbara. *Smoke and Ashes: The Story of the Holocaust*. New York: Holiday House, 1988.

Rossel, Seymour. *The Holocaust*. New York: Franklin Watts, 1981.

Rubin, Arnold. *The Evil Men Do: The Story of the Nazis*. New York: Julian Messner, 1977.

Schur, Maxine. *Hannah Szenes: A Song of Light*. Philadelphia: Jewish Publication Society, 1986.

Senesh, Hannah. *Hannah Senesh: Her Life and Diary*. New York: Schocken, 1972.

Stadtler, Bea. *The Holocaust: A History of Courage and Resistance*. New York: Behrman House, 1975.

Volavkova, Hana, ed. *I Never Saw Another Butterfly: Children's Drawings and Poems from Terezin Concentration Camp*. New York: Schocken, 1978.

Wiesel, Elie. *Night*. New York: Hill & Wang, 1969.

Zar, Rose. *In the Mouth of the Wolf*. Philadelphia: Jewish Publication Society, 1984.

Zieman, Joseph. *The Cigarette Sellers of the Three Crosses Square*. Minneapolis: Lerner Publications, 1975.

FICTION

Baer, Edith. *A Frost in the Night: A Girlhood on the Eve of the Third Reich*. New York: Pantheon, 1980.

Bergman, Tamar. *The Boy from Over There*. Translated from the Hebrew by Hillel Halkin. Boston: Houghton Mifflin, 1988.

Bishop, Claire Hucket. *Twenty and Ten*. New York: Viking, 1952.

Chaikin, Miriam. *Finders Weepers*. New York: Harper & Row, 1980.

Kerr, Judith. *When Hitler Stole Pink Rabbit*. New York: Coward, McCann & Geoghegan, 1972.

Suggested Reading

Levitan, Sonia. *Journey to America*. New York: Atheneum, 1970.

Levoy, Myron. *Allan and Naomi*. New York: Harper & Row, 1977.

Moskin, Marrietta. *I Am Rosemarie*. New York: John Day, 1972.

Orgel, Doris. *The Devil in Vienna*. New York: Dial, 1978.

Orlev, Uri. *The Island on Bird Street*. Boston: Houghton Mifflin, 1983.

Richter, Hans Peter. *Friedrich*. New York: Holt, Rinehart and Winston, 1970.

Sachs, Marilyn. *A Pocketful of Seeds*. New York: Doubleday, 1973.

Suhl, Yuri. *Uncle Misha's Partisans*. New York: Franklin Watts, 1975.

Van Slockum, Hilda. *Borrowed House*. New York: Farrar, Straus and Giroux, 1975.

Bibliography

A PARTIAL LISTING OF SOURCES

Adler, Stanislaw. *In the Warsaw Ghetto, 1940–1943: An Account of a Witness*. Jerusalem: Yad Vashem, 1982.

Arad, Yitzhak: Gutman, Yisrael, and Margaliot, Abraham, eds. *Documents on the Holocaust*. Jerusalem, Yad Vashem, 1981.

Bauer, Yehuda. *A History of the Holocaust*. New York: Franklin Watts, 1982.

Baynes, Norman H., ed. *The Speeches of Adolf Hitler*. New York: Howard Fertig, 1969.

Black, C. E., and Helmreich, E. C. *Twentieth Century Europe*. New York: Alfred A. Knopf, 1966.

Comay, Joan. *Who's Who in Jewish History*. New York: David McKay, 1974.

Davidson, Eugene. *The Making of Adolf Hitler*. New York: Macmillan, 1977.

    The Trial of the Germans. New York: Macmillan, 1966.

Dawidowicz, Lucy S. *On Equal Terms: Jews in America, 1881–1981*. New York: Holt, Rinehart and Winston, 1982.

    The War Against the Jews 1933–1945. New York: Holt, Rinehart and Winston, 1975.

Dimont, Max I. *The Indestructible Jews*. New York: New American Library, 1973.

Gilbert, Martin. *Final Journey*. New York: Mayflower, 1979.

    The Holocaust. New York: Holt, Rinehart, and Winston, 1985.

Bibliography

Goldston, Robert. *The Life and Death of Nazi Germany*. New York: Fawcett, 1967.

Henry, Frances. *Victims and Neighbors: A Small Town in Nazi Germany Remembered*. South Hadley, Massachusetts: Bergin and Garvey, 1984.

Hilberg, Raul. *The Destruction of the European Jews*. New York: Holmes and Meier, 1985.

Hitler, Adolf. *Mein Kampf*. Translated by Ralph Manheim. Boston: Houghton Mifflin, 1943.

The Holocaust. Jerusalem: Yad Vashem, 1975.

The Holocaust. New York: Garland, 1982.

Keller, Werner. *Diaspora: The Post-Biblical History of the Jews*. New York: Harcourt, Brace and World, 1966.

Kubizek, August. *The Young Hitler I Knew*. Westport, Connecticut: Greenwood, 1976.

Landman, Isaac, ed. *The Universal Jewish Encyclopedia*. New York: Universal Jewish Encyclopedia Company, 1948.

Leckie, Robert. *Delivered From Evil: The Saga of World War II*. New York: Harper & Row, 1987.

Lidz, Richard. *An Oral History of World War II*. New York: G.P. Putnam, 1980.

Lipstadt, Deborah E. *Beyond Belief*. New York: Free Press, 1986.

Maser, Werner. *Hitler: Legend, Myth and Reality*. Translated by Peter and Betty Ross. New York: Harper & Row, 1971.

Meed, Vladka. *On Both Sides of the Wall*. New York: Holocaust Library, 1979.

Morse, Arthur. *While Six Million Died: A Chronicle of American Apathy*. New York: Hart, 1975.

Plant, Richard. *The Pink Triangle*. New York: Henry Holt, 1986.

Poliakov, Leon. *Harvest of Hate*. New York: Holocaust Library, 1979.
Ringelblum, Emmanuel. *Notes from the Warsaw Ghetto*. New York: McGraw-Hill, 1958.

Roth, Cecil, ed. *Encyclopedia Judaica*. Jerusalem: Keter, 1972.

Segal, Nancy L. "Holocaust Twins: Their Special Bond." *Psychology Today*, August 1985, pp. 52–58.

Shirer, William L. *The Rise and Fall of the Third Reich*. New York: Simon and Schuster, 1960.

Snyder, Louis. *Encyclopedia of the Third Reich*. New York: McGraw-Hill, 1976.

Teaching About the Holocaust and Genocide, Volumes I and II. Albany: The University of the State of New York, 1985.

Bibliography

Thalmann, Rita, and Feinerman, Emmanuel. *Crystal Night*. New York: Coward, McCann & Geoghegan, 1974.

Thomas, Gordon, and Witts, Max Morgan. *Voyage of the Damned*. New York: Stein and Day, 1974.

Toland, John. *Adolf Hitler*. New York: Doubleday, 1976.

Trials of War Criminals Before the Nuernberg Military Tribunals: Nuernberg, October 1946–April 1949. Washington, D.C.: U.S. Government Printing Office, 1949.

Webb, Arnold. *The Holocaust: A Study of Genocide*. New York: Board of Education of the City of New York, Division of Curriculum and Instruction, 1979.

Wistrich, Robert, *Who's Who in Nazi Germany*. New York: Macmillan, 1982.

Wyman, David S. *The Abandonment of the Jews: America and the Holocaust 1941–1945*. New York: Pantheon, 1984.

Acknowledgments

The author wishes to thank Ms. Judith Levin of Yad Vashem, Jerusalem, for her help in locating many of the photographs used in this book.

Map on page ii prepared by Barry Varela.

The photographs in this book are from the following sources and are used with permission: National Archives, pages 5 (top), 27, 32, 49, 50, 106, 111 (bottom), 113, 116 (top), 116 (bottom). Raoul Wallenberg Committee of the United States, page 87 (top). Yad Vashem, pages 5 (bottom), 7, 8 (top), 9 (top), 9 (bottom), 11, 12 (bottom), 14 (top), 19, 20 (top), 22 (top), 28 (top), 29 (bottom), 31, 34, 35, 36 (top), 36 (bottom), 37, 40 (top), 44, 46, 48, 51, 52 (top), 53 (top), 54, 55, 57, 58, 60 (left), 60 (right), 61 (top), 61 (bottom), 63, 68, 69, 70, 72, 73, 74, 75, 80, 81, 83, 84, 85, 87 (bottom), 88 (top), 90, 91, 95, 97 (top), 97 (bottom), 98 (top), 102 (top), 102 (bottom), 103, 105, 107, 110, 111 (top), 114, 117 (top), 117 (bottom), 120, 122, 123, 124, 128.

All other photographs, including jacket photographs, are from private collections and are used with permission.

Index

Numbers in *italics* indicate pages with illustrations.

Index

Index

About the Author

David A. Adler is the author of more than eighty fiction and nonfiction works for young readers, including the Cam Jansen mysteries and biographies of Martin Luther King, Jr.; Thomas Jefferson; and George Washington. Among his books on Jewish subjects are *Our Golda: The Story of Golda Meir*, a Carter G. Woodson Honor Book; *A Picture Book of Jewish Holidays*, an ALA Notable Book; and a book for younger readers on the Holocaust, *The Number on My Grandfather's Arm*, winner of the Sydney Taylor Book Award.

David Adler is a senior editor at the Jewish Publication Society and lives in New York with his wife and family.